Appalachian Magazine
—Presents—
Mountain Superstitions, Ghost Stories & Haint Tales

A Collection of Memories & Commentaries from the Mountains of Appalachia

Copyright © 2018 StatelyTies Media

All rights reserved.

ISBN: 9781726866231

DEDICATION

This publication is lovingly dedicated to the countless number of Appalachian coal miners, granny women and children of the mountains who have been misunderstood for centuries, but still endure.

Appalachian Magazine is committed to serving as a living monument to the incredible lives of the men and women who call Appalachia home.

Appalachian Magazine
Travel, History, Life.

We'd Love to Hear From You:

Tell us what you think of our publication, schedule us for a speaking engagement or simply follow us on social media so that you never miss a new article!

Send us an Email: publisher@appalachianmagazine.com

Facebook: Facebook.com/AppalachianMagazine

Twitter: @AppalachianMag

Appalachian Magazine: Our Story

How we were started

In December 2013, West Virginia native Jeremy T.K. Farley launched a blog sharing the many stories he had heard his grandparents recount of life in the coal mining towns of Mingo County. Within three months of the site's original launch, more than 3,000 people had subscribed to receive updates from the online publication and within a matter of days, *Appalachian Magazine* was born. Initially, just a blog he and his wife updated on a weekly basis, *Appalachian Magazine* has grown into one of the region's premier culture, history and travel publications, showcasing the Appalachian region's rich heritage, as well as the many businesses committed to moving the economy forward. Today, Appalachian Magazine has over 100,000 Facebook fans and more than a half-million monthly readers.

Our Mission & Passion

Being a native of Appalachia (Appa-LATCH-uh), Jeremy has a passion for the mountains, its people and history. This passion is felt in every article published on the website or printed in the bi-annual hardcopy edition of the magazine.

"The purpose of Appalachian Magazine is to showcase the tourism opportunities, rich history and timeless lifestyle of the greater-Appalachian region, while at the same time, providing a platform for frank and honest dialogue regarding the areas where improvement is needed."

The number of writers featured in both the online and print publication is ever growing and as the publication moves into the next phase of its existence, we remain committed to fulfilling our mission statement.

Are We Naturally Superstitious?
Written by Emma May Buckingham
Published in 1906

The wisest amongst us would probably be astonished at the number of tolerably well educated people who believe in prognostics, dreams, superstitions, old saws, and unlucky days. There are thousands of men and women today who think as their grandmothers did a century ago: that it forebodes ill luck to see the new moon over the left shoulder, that it is wrong to start on a journey or commence a new piece of work on Friday — while the majority of the people in our rural districts, learned and unlearned, place great stress upon the signs of the Zodiac. Their planting, sowing, grafting fruit trees, transplanting, weeding, reaping, mowing, pruning vines and setting their fowls must be done during certain phases of the moon when the sign is right.

Mothers wean their babies, cut their children's hair and pick their geese only when the moon is new. Housewives boil soap or plant flower and vegetable gardens also when the moon is in a certain quarter while their husbands and brothers fish, shear sheep and do a hundred other things according to the sign lore of their ancestors.

Certain events occurring in the old of the moon such as births are said by the above named class to cause ill luck.

There are hundreds of intelligent people in our cities, as well as in the country, who will start and turn pale at the sound of the death watch or the howling of a dog; while tens of thousands believe that to dream of blood or losing teeth or crossing a muddy stream or talking with or seeing friends who have long been dead or absent is a fore runner of death, the loss of a friend, or of certain disaster.

Others believe that to forget something and go back after it is the sign of a fast coming accident, while fifty percent of our housekeepers see trouble looming up ahead of them whenever their bread cracks open in the middle, or a looking glass is broken, or a picture falls from the wall no matter how old or moth-eaten the cord may have been which had held it.

One of the most sensible old ladies I ever knew in other things was in the habit of saying, "My right eye brow itches: There is a man coming here" or "My left eye brow itches: Some woman is coming today to see me." or "My ear rings dreadful loud: We shall hear of a death soon."

She would say, "My nose itches, I shall be angry at someone before night," and "My left ear burns, somebody is talking about me."

And when I would laugh at the dear old soul and try to reason her out of such nonsense, she would declare that she never knew such signs to fail.

Many intelligent people believe that it presages disaster to meet a hearse. They tell us that it is wrong to watch a friend out of sight after one has said good bye.

An educated lady says, "Plants will not grow if you thank the donor for them – neither will seeds."

A goodly number of the world's most enlightened inhabitants look with apprehension at an approaching comet, for according to the popular belief, comets have predicted war plagues and national troubles in all the ages of the past.

We know that astrology, witchcraft, sooth saying, and miracles are now considered exploded ideas; things of a past era, yet there are many in our own land and times who say that people are possessed of good as well as evil spirits.

There are others who have faith in the charlatans who profess that they can pray fire out of burns and pow wow away diseases. Fortune telling still lives in all civilized countries.

We daily hear of faith cures and miraculous interventions in spite of our boasted civilization. The Chinese believe that the souls of the dead come back and partake of the good things which their surviving friends set out for them on holidays and anniversary occasions, while the army of spiritualists with their mediums, séance, seers, and spiritual clairvoyants tell us that they hold communication with the spirits of those who have departed from this earth life continually.

The murderer who sees the ghosts of his victims, the engineer who nightly imagines that the spirits of those whom he has killed accidentally appear to him, and the ghosts of unkind words to the dying or of lost opportunities to do good are not the only shades that our poets sing about.

Black cats have long been associated with superstitions, though not all were negative. The Scots believed the arrival of an unknown black cat to one's house was a sign of prosperity. Photo courtesy of "DrL"

One of the most intelligent writers of the nineteenth century said "There are more ghosts at table than the host's invited…"

Many people believe in warnings that serve as premonitions of death. They will tell you that they always hear unaccountable noises before the death of dear friends. We all know that at times the wisest and most skeptical among us approach very near the border land of the unexplainable, if not supernatural. Mysterious sights and sounds and appearances, as well as experiences, have occasionally defied reason herself and put our credulity to the hardest tests imaginable.

Are we all more or less superstitious? Did not the great Napoleon Bonaparte believe in his star of destiny, also in unlucky and lucky days? The origin of bad signs dated back to antiquity.

The spilling of salt on the table is considered a very bad omen because it is emblematic of friendship and hospitality and spilling it is a sure sign of a quarrel or disrupture of friendly relations.

The seating of 13 at table is currently believed to be an omen of death to one of the guests even in this twentieth century.

***

The premise of Emma May Buckingham's 1906 article is just as relevant some 112 years later as it was the day she first penned it. Though many of the precise superstitions of which she spoke have largely fallen out of use, humanity is still given to the paranormal and unexplainable – and here in the Appalachian highlands, we are no different..

The mission of Appalachian Magazine is to honestly document the peculiar events, customs, and beliefs of our ancestors for the benefit of our posterity as well as humanity. This print edition seeks to do just this, by highlighting the fascinating superstitions, ghost stories and haint tales of the mountains – you don't have to believe them or even like them, but these stories have defined who we are as a people.

—*Part One*—
Haints, Spells & Mountain Living

Setting the Stage:
Mountain Religion, Illiteracy and The Bible

As an Appalachian pastor who has spent the better part of two decades ministering in too many mountain churches to count in the hills of Southwest Virginia, Eastern Kentucky, East Tennessee and Southern West Virginia, I am more than well aware of the role religion plays in the day to day life of the communities I have dedicated my life to serving.

From the moment I was born on a sweltering summer's night in Logan County, West Virginia, overlooking the Guyandotte River, until the day I take my final breath, these people are my own and I am unashamed of the accent they have entrusted to me or the eternal faith that dwells inside me thanks to their preaching.

With this being said, I am also acutely cognizant of the reality that locked away somewhere in our mountain DNA is a "By Gawd, I'll do this my way," mentality – a temperament that I have both despised in others, while at the same time championed in myself.

This character trait of thinking for ourselves and being unafraid to go against the grain has through the years been both a blessing and a curse. It has also left us ostracized – our neighbors to the north look at us and laugh at our backwards ways, while our neighbors in Dixie have somewhat accepted us into their "red state" club as an honorary member, knowing that the shaky alliance between the Old South and the mountaineers won't last forever; after all, the last time the North and the South battled, we largely remained neutral – or selected one of the two sides out of necessity, but never out of a true alliance.

To put it simply, in the mountains of Appalachia, we march to our own beat, and we're mighty proud of this.

Perhaps nowhere is the beat to which we march as distinctive as it is when it comes to our religion.

A simple drive along US Route 52 through McDowell County, West Virginia, will reveal a plethora of non-denomination, locally devised, houses of worship, with names that range from "The Only True Church" to "Signs & Wonders to Follow".

Interestingly, the high level of respect and reverence our ancestors held for the Word of God was bested only by many, by their lack of understanding of that same Book – This point was well made in Richard Davids' 1970 book, *The Man Who Moved a Mountain*, a book that is in my opinion the best work ever written about Appalachia!

From my experiences "peddling religion", as one local politician accused me of doing not too long ago, the vast majority of the people living in the Bible Belt, at least in 2018, have a strong reverence and respect for that old black Book that sits in some dusty corner shelf of their home – even believing it contains the key to eternal life and earthly happiness; sadly, however, very few have ever dedicated any length of time to actually reading and studying this Book – still, so many stand ready to argue its premises, objectives and standards without hesitation.

The combination of having a great respect and reverence for such a profound Book, as well as having so little an understanding of this same manuscript's commands and statements has largely led to the creation of so many of the superstitions that have defined previous generations of Appalachian residents and still shows its face even today.

***

The following words were written by Pennsylvania-born travel writer, Horace Kephart in the year 1913. Though I am far from being a fan of Kephart's work due to the arrogant and superior tone he so often reveals when writing about Appalachia, I can conclude that when it came to religion, Kephart seemed to have hit the nail square on the head when describing many of our ancestors – and it is for these very reasons outlined below that a culture developed in the hills of Appalachia, a century ago, of a hybrid form of Christianity mixed with superstition, haints and witchery.

Horace Kephart: ***Our Southern Highlanders, 1913:***

Most of the mountain preachers nowadays denounce dances and play parties as sinful diversions, though their real objection seems to be that such gatherings are counter attractions that thin out the religious ones. Be that as it may, they certainly have put a damper on frolics so that in very many mountain settlements, "goin to meetin'" is recognized primarily as a social function and affords almost the only chance for recreation in which family can join family without restraint.

Meetings are held in the log schoolhouse. The congregation ranges itself men on one side, women on the other, on rude benches that sometimes have no backs. Everybody goes. If one judged from attendance, he would rate our highlanders as the most religious people in America. This impression is strengthened in a stranger, by the grave and astoundingly patient attention that is given an illiterate – or nearly illiterate – minister while he holds forth for two or three mortal hours on the beauties of predestination, freewill, foreordination, immersion, foot washing, or on the delinquencies of them "acorn fed critters that has gone 'New Light' over in Cope's Cove."

After an al fresco lunch, everybody doggedly returns to hear another circuit rider expound and denounce at the top of his voice until late afternoon "as long as the spirit lasts" and he has "good wind."

When he warms up, he throws in a gasping "ah" or "uh" at short intervals, which constitutes the "holy tone".

Doctor MacClintock gives this example, "Oh brethren, repent ye, and repent ye of your sins, ah, fer if ye don't, ah, the Lord, ah, he will grab yer by the seat of yer pants, ah, and held yer over hell fire till ye holler like a coon!"

During these services, there is a good deal of running in and out by the men and boys, most of whom gradually congregate on the outside to whittle, gossip, drive bargains, and debate among themselves some point of dogma that is too good to keep still about. Nearly all of our highlanders from youth upward show an amazing fondness for theological dispute… I have known two or three hundred mountain lumber jacks, hard swearing and hard drinking, tough as they make 'ems to be whetted to a fighting edge over the rocky problem, "Was Saul damned? Can a suicide enter the kingdom of heaven?"

The mountaineers are intensely universally Protestant. You will seldom find a backwoodsman who knows what a Roman Catholic is. As John Fox says, "He is the only man in the world whom the Catholic Church has made little or no effort to proselyte."

Dislike of Episcopalianism is still strong among people who do not know, or pretend not to know, what the word means. "Any Episcopalians around here?" asked a clergyman at a mountain cabin.

"I don't know," said the old woman.

"Jim's got the skins of a lot o' varmints up in the loft. Mebbe you can find one up thar."

The first settlers of Appalachia mainly were Presbyterians as became Scotch Irishmen, but they fell away from that faith partly because the wilderness was too poor to support a regular ministry and partly because it was too democratic for Calvinism, with its supreme authority of the clergy… the mountaineer retains a passion for hair splitting argument over points of doctrine and the cocksure intolerance of John Knox, but the ancestral creed itself has been forgotten.

The circuit rider, whether Methodist or Baptist, found here a field ripe for his harvest. Being himself, self-supporting and unassuming, he won easily the confidence of the people. He preached a highly emotional religion that worked his audience into the ecstasy that [the] people love. And he introduced a mighty agent of evangelization among outdoor folk when he started the camp meeting.

The season for camp meetings is from mid-August to October. The festival may last a week in one place. It is a jubilee week to the work-worn and home chained women, their only diversion from a year of unspeakably monotonous toil. And for the young folks it is their theater, their circus, their county fair – I say this with no disrespect, "big meetin' time" is a gala week, if there be any such thing at all in the mountains, its attractiveness is full as much secular as spiritual to the great body of the people. It is a camp by day only or up to closing time; no mountaineer owns a tent.

Preachers and exhorters are housed nearby and visitors from all the country scatter about with their friends or sleep in the open, cooking their meals by the wayside. In these backwoods revival meetings, we can witness to day the weird phenomena of ungovernable shouting, ecstasy, bodily contortions, trance catalepsy, and other results of hypnotic suggestion and the contagious one mindedness of an overwrought crowd. This is called "taking a big through" and is regarded as the madness of supernatural joy. It is a mild form of that extraordinary frenzy which swept the Kentucky settlements in 1800 when thousands of men and women at the camp meetings fell victims to the jerks, barking exercises, erotic vagaries, physical wreckage or insanity to which the frenzy led."

PHOTO: Typical mountain camp meeting gathering.

Many [have been] easily carried away by new doctrines, extravagantly presented. Religious mania is taken for inspiration by the superstitious who are looking for signs and wonders.

At one time, Mormon prophets lured women from the backwoods of western Carolina and eastern Tennessee.

Later there was a similar exodus of people to the Castellites, a sect of whom it was commonly remarked that everybody who joins the Castellites goes crazy.

In a feud town of eastern Kentucky, not long ago, I saw two Holiness exhorters prancing before a solemnly attentive crowd in the courthouse square, one of them shouting and exhibiting the holy laugh, while the other pointed to the Cumberland River and cried, "I don't say if I had the faith, I say 'I have the faith' to walk over that river dry shod."

I scanned the crowd and saw nothing but belief or willingness to believe on any countenance.

Of course most mountaineers are more intelligent than that, but few of them are free from superstitions of one kind or other.

There are today many believers in witchcraft among them, though none own it to any, but their intimates, and nearly everybody in the hills has faith in portents.

The mountain clergy as a general rule are hostile to book larnin, "for there ain't no Holy Ghost in it."

One of them who had spent three months at a theological school told President Frost, "Yes, the seminary is a good place ter go and git rested up, but tain't worth-while fer me ter go thar no more's — long as I've got good wind."

In general, the religion of the mountaineers has little influence on every day behavior, little to do with the moral law.

Salvation is by faith alone and not by works. Sometimes a man is churched for breaking the Sabbath, cuss'in, tale bearin, but sins of the flesh are rarely punished, being regarded as amiable frailties of mankind.

One of our old timers nonchalantly admitted in court that he and a preacher had marked a false corner tree which figured in an important land suit.

On cross examination he was asked, "You admit that you and Preacher X forged that corner tree? Didn't you give Preacher X a good character in your testimony? Do you consider it consistent with his profession as a minister of the Gospel to forge corner trees?"

"Aw," replied the witness, "religion ain't got nothin' to do with corner trees."

John Fox relates that "A feud leader who had about exterminated the opposing faction and had made a good fortune for a mountaineer while doing it, for he kept his men busy getting out timber when they weren't fighting, said to me in all seriousness, 'I have triumphed agin' my enemies time and time agin. The Lord's on my side and I gits a better and better Christian ever year."

A preacher riding down a ravine came upon an old mountaineer hiding in the bushes with his rifle.

"What are you doing there my friend?"

"Ride on stranger," was the easy answer.

"I'm a waitin fer Jim Johnson and with the help of the Lawd, I'm goin to blow his damn head off."

***

The preceding commentary on mountain religion of a century ago is inline with the words provided by other writers from the same period and showcases a form of Christianity that places far more admiration and trust in the emotion and showmanship of religion than in the doctrines and precepts laid out in its authoritative Book. Therefore, superstition flourished in the hills a century ago and a half ago, and aided by the mysterious forces of the dark Appalachian woodlands, witchery, hauntings and sorcery were permitted to exist alongside Christianity in a way that has seldom been allowed elsewhere in the world — creating one of the most fascinating cultures the world has ever known.

Remembering the Days of Granny Women, Root Workers & Witch Doctors

Granny Women

Not many days after first arriving in the New World, the fiercely independent Scots-Irish got to work putting as many miles between themselves and the ruling elite as possible. They despised government and distrusted most everyone – especially the privileged and wealthy gentry who made their homes back east by the ocean.

Undeterred by the great unknown, these original adventurers pressed west, moving deeper into the dense and dark virgin forests of the Appalachian Mountains.

The world they would discover was unlike anything that had been seen previously nor would be again seen with human eyes: walls of steep mountains protected by lush and fertile valleys, trees 45 ft. wide, mountain lions that would stalk surveying parties for days and some of the most unforgiving landscape in the entire New World.

Though their contemporaries regarded life at such a remote outpost most wretched, the men and women who opted to settle the Blue Ridge in the bloody and haunted mountains of old could not have been more pleased with their new homes — the sheer remoteness and inaccessibility of their homesteads was selling point enough; even if living the lifestyle would require one to do so at unspeakably great peril.

In the days that followed, the young girls who had first crossed into the region by foot with their parents would become brides of one of the few boys they had ever known. And naturally, not long after this, another generation of fearsome and rugged mountain people would be born... Provided they could make it past that most critical hurdle of all, childbirth.

Though there are no official counts, we know that the birthing process often resulted in tears of great sadness in the dank woods of yesteryear, leading a countless multitude of young women to early graves.

The handful of women who were fortunate enough to survive childbirth and then successfully keep their own children alive often became highly respected members of early Appalachian communities, becoming affectionately known as "Granny Women".

At a time and in a culture where books were scarce and far away, the life's experiences and acquired knowledge of Granny Women became a commodity in great demand — first as a midwife and birthing coach and later as a full-fledged medical professional. A professional who had never stepped a single foot into any school, but one whose knowledge of herbs and "healing ticks" were second to none.

Separating themselves from other medical workers, Granny Women fancied themselves to not have expected or received payment for their services and were viewed as critical elements to mountain life.

In 1921, John C. Campbell wrote about the remaining Granny Women of Appalachia:

"There is something magnificent in many of the older women with their stern theology—part mysticism, part fatalism—and their deep understanding of life. Patience, endurance, and resignation are written in the close-set mouth and in the wrinkles about the eyes; but the eyes themselves are kindly, full of interest, not unrelieved by a twinkling appreciation of pleasant things. 'Granny'

"'Granny' —and one may be a grandmother young in the mountains—if she has survived the labor and tribulation of her younger days, has gained a freedom and a place of irresponsible authority in the home hardly rivaled by the men of the family. Her grown sons pay to her an attention which they do not always accord their wives; and her husband, while he remains still undisputed master of the home, defers to her opinion to a degree unknown in her younger days. Her daughters and her grandchildren she frankly rules. Though superstitious she has a fund of common sense, and she is a shrewd judge of character. In sickness, she is the first to be consulted, for she is generally something of an herb doctor, and her advice is sought by the young people of half the countryside in all things from a love affair to putting a new web in the loom.

Photo: November 1933, "Aunt Lizzie Reagan weaving old-fashioned jean at the Pi Beta Phi school, Gatlinburg, Tennessee. This aged mountain woman lives near the school and earns her living weaving." Courtesy of Tennessee Valley Authority.

Like today, Appalachian women from a century ago were among the strongest and most industrious women in America.

"It is not surprising if she is something of a pessimist on the subject of marriage. 'Don't you never get married' is advice that is more than likely to pass her lips."

Many of these Granny Women's words of wisdom have been lost to time, but chances are that the majority of our readers are far more familiar with some of these women's words of wisdom than we may initially care to admit. Thanks to these women, we all grew with the understanding that the cure for an earache is urine!

The eventual downfall of Granny Women came when medical professionals were dispatched into the Appalachian Mountains by their state governments around the turn of the previous century in order to better educate the people on childbirth practices, as well as fundamental medical knowledge.

A 1914 edition of the *Kentucky Medical Journal* gave a precursor of what would shape to be one of the most underreported Appalachian feuds in history, local Granny Women vs. "all 'em know nut'n doctors".

The medical professionals accused Granny Women of causing needless anxieties to expectant mothers by propagating a belief in the superstitious idea of maternal impression.

Known in the mountains as "blood feeling", maternal impression was a belief that a sudden fear of some object or animal in a pregnant woman would cause her child to bear the mark of that object of fear, i.e., snake, mouse, raging river or lightning, etc.

The journal lambasted doctors serving in the region for not standing up to the strong and respected Granny Women, "It matters not what character of mark or deformity may be found on a babe, the mother can look back over the nine months and think of something that the mark reminds her of, then with a firm belief in this superstition, it is easy for her to believe that her babe was marked by maternal impression. Then, with a physician who has not backbone enough to go up against the opinion of the granny woman and explain this fallacy, is it any wonder the neighbor's wife across the street will spend the remainder of her gestation in abject horror and fear for her own babe that is yet unborn?"

Witch Doctors

The individuals who would eventually become known as Witch Doctors got their start much like Granny Women: serving as a form of mountain healer in an era and area where doctors and medical knowledge was scarce.

Though their Granny Women counterparts offered wisdom and medical treatment for physical ailments rooted in superstition, Witch Doctors in the woods of Appalachia grew to focus almost entirely upon treating physical ailments believed to have been caused by witchcraft.

In its original meaning, Witch Doctors were emphatically not witches themselves, but rather people who had remedies to protect others against witchcraft.

Charles Mackay's book, *Extraordinary Popular Delusions and the Madness of Crowds*, first published in 1841, attests to the practice of belief in Witch Doctors in England at the time:

"In the north of England, the superstition lingers to an almost inconceivable extent. Lancashire abounds with witch-doctors, a set of quacks, who pretend to cure diseases inflicted by the devil. The practices of these worthies may be judged of by the following case, reported in the *Hertford Reformer*, of the 23rd of June, 1838. The witch-doctor alluded to is better known by the name of the cunning man, and has a large practice in the counties of Lincoln and Nottingham. According to the writer in *The Reformer*, the dupe, whose name is not mentioned, had been for about two years afflicted with a painful abscess and had been prescribed for without relief by more than one medical gentleman. He was urged by some of his friends, not only in his own village but in neighbouring ones, to consult the witch-doctor, as they were convinced he was under some evil influence. He agreed and sent his wife to the cunning man, who lived in New Saint Swithin's, in Lincoln. She was informed by this ignorant impostor that her husband's disorder was an infliction of the devil, occasioned by his next-door neighbours, who had made use of certain charms for that purpose. From the description he gave of the process, it appears to be the same as that employed by Dr. Fian and Gellie Duncan, to work woe upon King James. He stated that the neighbours, instigated by a witch, whom he pointed out, took some wax, and moulded it before the fire into the form of her husband, as near as they could represent him; they then pierced the image with pins on all sides – repeated the Lord's Prayer backwards, and offered prayers to the devil that he would fix his stings into the person whom that figure represented, in like manner as they pierced it with pins.

"To counteract the effects of this diabolical process, the witch-doctor prescribed a certain medicine, and a charm to be worn next to the body, on that part where the disease principally lay. The patient was to repeat the 109th and 119th Psalms every day, or the cure would not be effectual. The fee which he claimed for this advice was a guinea."

The belief and faith in Witch Doctors was especially rampant in the wilderness across the Atlantic in America.

In 1924, James Watt Raine retold some of the first-hand stories he had heard Appalachian mountain people tell, including the use of Witch Doctors:

"Old Doc was a-walkin' along with his wife. They was both elderly. She said, 'Let's go up to this house and git a light for our pipes.' (Folks didn't have matches – none to speak of – in them days; many a time I've walked a mile to a neighbor's with a shovel to borrow fire.) Well, they found a child thar screamin' and kick' – be witched. Doc told 'em to git him nine new pins that hadn't never been stuck in cloth and a bottle. He putt the pins in the bottle and set it on the fireboard (Mantel-Shelf). Then he got a shingle and drew a picture of a witch-woman and told the man to set it up agin a stump and shoot it jest at sundown. About a week later that Doc was comin' by agin, and he inquired atter the child. Hit were all right. Then he axed had anybody died suddintly, and they told him an old woman across the valley had died with a shriek, ever when the man shot the picture with his rifle-gun. And the bottle on the fireboard busted into a thousand pieces, and they never did find ary on of the pins."

While most Americans believe the Salem Witch Trials from the 1600s represented a long forgotten era in American history in which neighbors would out of superstition and suggestion accuse each other of being witches, the sad reality is that less than a century ago, Appalachian women were being falsely accused and ostrized due to the mere accusation from a Witch Doctor of them being a witch.

One contemporary writers stated that anyone who lived differently or peculiar ran the risk of being accused of practicing black magic:

"Any one possessed of occult attainments, living differently from others, engaged in unprofitable and incomprehensible occupations, becomes a suspect. The people live in dread of spells and terrific appearances and supernaturalism affords an explanation for everything not understood.

"It is quite proper and satisfactory surely that if a girl wishes to know whether her future husband will be a stranger or come from the vicinity, she can find out by going alone and at night, on New Year's Eve, standing silently by a peach tree and shaking its stem. Should a dog bark, her suitor comes from a distance, but if a cock crows, his home is near.

"It is necessary to wait until spring in order to ascertain his complexion: Then when the first dove comes she must take off her shoes, turn round three times. Then again by the course of the sun and inspect her stockings. The color of any hair found adhering to them will be the same as his.

"How long marriage is to be delayed the earliest whippoorwill reveals. The number of times this bird's notes are repeated, mark intervening years" all thanks to the instructions of the local Witch Doctor.

Root Worker

While Granny Women and Witch Doctors were busy conjuring cures and offering advice grounded in sorcery to pregnant mothers and troubled farmers in the forgotten hills of Appalachia, farther to the south, another group of mysterious witches were being employed by both whites and blacks to provide prophesies and spells, especially regarding love.

These men came to be known as "Root Workers" and their form of witchcraft is a form of hoodoo.

Hoodoo, a form of spirituality developed among Southern slaves incorporates a number of West African spiritual traditions and beliefs, but was also heavily influenced by Native American practices, as well as French and Christian customs.

Prior to the American Civil War, Hoodoo religious practices were held in secret far away from white slave owners; however, following the war's end and the abolition of slavery, southern blacks migrated north in what became known as the Great Migration.

The Great Migration moved many Root Workers into northern cities, as well as the coalfields of Appalachia, providing an opportunity to introduce the West African form of witchcraft to the people of the mountains.

***

In 1906, J.H. Smith described a Root Worker in his book, "Maudelle: A Novel Founded on Facts Gathered from Living Witnesses". Although distrusting of the Root Workers' motives or sincerity, Smith's words offer great insight as to how these Southern witches would fuction:

[Because of the] belief in ghosts in the minds of the poor whites, he has a large following of whites who believe in conjuration witchcraft and fortune telling. The cunning negro conjurer manages somehow to turn his eyes red, and with a pair of red eyes, as a native, he exerts a wonderful influence over black and white.

Very frequently young white men and girls seek the aid of the root worker in complicated cases of love affairs. The conjurer always keeps a great number of little packages or bottles in stock, known as a hand, which range in price from twenty-five cents to five-dollars, according to the gravity of the case to be treated. A hand consists of parts of a dried snake and lizard, various roots, earth from a grave, and pieces of bone of a dead human being.

If any person or persons has enemies whom he wishes to injure, the conjurer prepares what is known as a throw. The throw is a preparation of roots and powders of dried reptiles, liquids, etc. which are to be planted in the path or under the door step of the enemy.

If the enemy is not brought down according to the promise of the conjurer, the failure is charged to the interference of some other conjurer at work for the enemy. In a case of this kind, a stronger throw has to be compounded and, of course, a considerably larger fee exacted.

A very large majority of whites and blacks wear luck bags about the neck. The famous rabbit foot is a negro conjurer's invention, notwithstanding, I have heard of the credit going to others.

Those who believe in such things live a life of constant uneasiness, as they are tossed back and forth between the signs of good and bad luck, hoping in one and fearing the other.

The Witches of Appalachia

The Bible, that old sacred Book which supremely ruled the lives of so many in the Appalachian mountainsides a century and a half ago, leaves no question concerning its take regarding witchcraft, sorcery and necromancy:

There shall not be found among you any one that maketh his son or his daughter to pass through the fire, or that useth divination, or an observer of times, or an enchanter, or a witch. Or a charmer, or a consulter with familiar spirits, or a wizard, or a necromancer. For all that do these things are an abomination unto the Lord: and because of these abominations the Lord thy God doth drive them out from before thee.
– Deuteronomy 18.10-12

Whether it was in spite of these verses or because of these verses, we may never know, but belief in witchcraft and tales of their sordid deeds abounded in the hollers of yesteryear. Not too long ago, one didn't need to look too far to find someone who either knew how to conjure up a spell or knew how to summon a charm that would prevent a spell from taking 'ah root.

***

In 1913, Appalachian native Josiah Henry Combs (1886-1960) published a book detailing life in Eastern Kentucky, "The Kentucky Highlanders from a Native Mountaineer's Viewpoint". His work was published in an era of exaggerated news reports and when national mockery of Appalachian people was rampant – he had hoped his book would record the true lives of Appalachian people for posterity; void of any prejudices either way.

Below is his published account and description of witches in the Kentucky mountains:

Many curious Old English customs and superstitions still persist in the Kentucky mountains. Some of the prevailing superstitious beliefs are as follows:

- Take a small stone from the creek bed and place it in the bottom of the grate or fire place and the hawks will cease catching the chickens.
- It is bad luck to start somewhere and turn back.
- Friday is an unlucky day.
- If a spirit or ghost pursues you, stop in the middle of some stream

and make the sign of the Cross with your fingers.
- If you kill a toad your cows will give bloody milk.

There are many charms for making one love you:
- Take the paddle of a goose's foot, boil it and give the water to your girl.
- When you hear a hen crow, kill her at once – for it is bad luck to allow her to live.
- When roosters crow at night, it is a sign that somebody has just died.
- Don't go to bed singing, for if you do, you will die during the night.
- There is no need of being bothered with warts, because any old woman possessed of supernatural powers can remove them for so many pins.
- Don't carry any farming implement through the house for it is bad luck.
- If you step over a grave in a graveyard or cemetery you will be the next person to be buried there.
- When a family moves to a different house or locality, it is bad luck to take a cat with them.
- If a child's finger nails are trimmed or pared before it is a year old, it will be guilty of stealing.
- If you look upward and count a hundred stars before lowering your head, you will drop dead before taking another step.
- If a bird flies into a house, it is a sign that someone in that family will die soon.

The casual observer as well as the student of folklore would suppose the idea of witchcraft died out with the persecution of witches at Salem, Massachusetts, at the close of the seventeenth century. But it did not die.

Less than fifty years ago, the belief in Witchcraft had quite a following in the Kentucky mountains. Nor has it died out yet. There are numbers and numbers of women and men in the mountains who are credited with the powers of witchcraft and who believe themselves to be gifted with those strange powers.

Usually they are persons who are past the medium station in years. The process by which one may become a witch or a wizard is weird and gruesome and offers a striking comparison to the old and familiar Faustus Legend.

The aspirant goes early in the morning before sunrise to the top of an adjacent mountain. Here, he or she hurls an anathema at Jehovah, owns the Devil as a master, then holds up a white handkerchief in front of the rising sun, shoots through it with a silver bullet, and blood drips down from it.

The operation is then complete and Dr. Faustus is beaten at his own game – these witches empowered with Satanic attributes cause a great deal of fear and trembling in a community.

Those who have been bewitched or who have had some of their domesticated animals bewitched are very anxious to court the favor of the witches. It is a common occurrence for these witches and wizards to metamorphose themselves into the form of a black cat when they go about their mischief making.

> **The Faustus Legend**
>
> Faust is a classic German legend, based on the historical Johann Georg Faust (c. 1480–1540). The erudite Faust is highly successful yet dissatisfied with his life, which leads him to make a pact with the Devil, exchanging his soul for unlimited knowledge and worldly pleasures.

Here are some of the things witches do:

They transform certain individuals into horses and ride them all night, restoring the bewitched to their natural shapes before daylight… his rational attributes remain intact throughout his transformation and he often complains of long difficult journeys, jumping of ditches, fences, etc.

Cows are often bewitched and their owners complain that they are not giving down milk, whereas the cows belonging to witches are continually yielding a plentiful supply. Even a churn and its contents can be bewitched and in order to break the spell, a coir of fifty cents is placed in the bottom of the churn before beginning to churn.

But a witch doesn't even have to own a cow in order to have plenty of butter at her own command. She occupies the remarkable and convenient distinction of being able to produce the creamy substance by merely squeezing the handle of an ordinary table fork.

Painful accidents sometimes befall witches:

Many years ago a man's wife, who was a witch, went one night to attend a meeting of the witches.

In the guise of a black cat, she came home to where her husband was sitting by the fireside and threw her paws upon his knees. Not especially in love with the salutation of this strange visitor, he chopped one of her paws off and immediately the hand of a woman lay upon his knee.

The next morning, his wife complained of sickness and was not disposed to get out of bed. The husband was suspicious and asked her to reach out her right arm. She did so and the hand was missing.

Now since so many people and animals are bewitched, there must be many charms to ward off witchcraft, and also doctors to [heal] against witches.

The witch hair ball is a dangerous weapon in the hands of witches. It is made by rolling a small bunch of hair from a horse or cow into a hard round ball. A witch can kill a person with one of these balls.

In Knott County, once upon a time, a wizard became jealous of another man. This man was plowing in his field one day and suddenly dropped dead between his plow handles. The case was investigated and it was found that the wizard had done the deed in this wise: He went into the woods, drew a picture of his enemy upon a tree, took aim with a gun and sent the witch ball through the picture.

It developed later that when the dead man fell between the plow handles, a witch ball dropped out of his mouth.

If a person or brute is being bewitched and a witch doctor's work begins, to tell the witch, at once [the tattler] begins to suffer great physical agony.

If the witch comes bearing a gift to the bewitched person or to the owner of the bewitched animal, if the gift is accepted, the work of the doctor or of the charm at once loses its efficacy.

When a witch is at her mischief making, she is invisible to everybody save to the person bewitched. She is invulnerable, even her heels, except when shot with a silver bullet by the hand of the bewitched.

Tennessee's Only Witch Trial Proceedings

The section below was written by Albert Ross Hogue in a book published in 1916, documenting the history of Fentress County, Tennessee.

Fifteen or twenty years ago the following appeared as a news item under the above head in the *Chattanooga Times*:

The official records have been received in this city as a matter of historical interest of the first and only arrest and prosecution for witchcraft ever had in Tennessee.

The scene was Jamestown, Fentress County claimed by many to be the Obedstown of Mark Twain and by many of the older residents to be the actual birthplace of Mark Twain, whose father was at one time Circuit Court Clerk of Fentress County and a practicing lawyer at the bar. The case of witchcraft was in the year 1835 and originated on the banks of the Obeys River, the trial being before Joshua Owens a Justice of the Peace.

An old man named Stout who lived in a very quiet way in the neighborhood, who did not attend church, who had been sitting up late at nights reading strange books and about whose early history nothing was known, was suspected of being a witch and when a daughter of one Taylor was taken violently ill with a disease that the doctor could not diagnose, it was determined to arrest old man Stout for bewitching her.

A large posse was secured and guns were loaded with silver bullets as it was thought that nothing else would kill a witch. The old man was arrested and brought to trial before Squire Owens.

A vast array of witnesses testified as to his habits and added that they had seen him escape from dwelling houses through the keyhole in the doors and that he had thrown people and animals into strange spells by his influence when they were miles away from him.

The officers and posse subjected him to a great many indignities and he was held to await the action of the grand jury. When court convened, Judge Abraham Caruthers, who was on the bench, and Gen. Jno. B. McCormick, the prosecuting attorney, refused to indict the old man; the action of the court and attorney general almost precipitated a riot in the court room.

Old man Stout then sued the officers and posse for damages and they pleaded as a defense that they were in the act of arraigning a criminal and cited the statute of Henry VIII and James I, making witchcraft a felony, which they declared had never been repealed in Tennessee.

Judge Caruthers, however, charged the jury that these statutes were repugnant to and destructive of the freedom of the State and to a republican form of government and by the Act of 1778, never in effect in Tennessee. Thus ended the first trial of a person charged with witchcraft in Tennessee by the conviction of the persons who had arrested him and subjected him to great indignities.

The above article was clipped from *the Times* and preserved by the author. The statements with reference to the facts in the case and the charge and action of the court are undoubtedly in the main true, but cannot be verified by the records in the Circuit Clerk's office – the records covering this period are missing. They were probably burned in the fire which consumed the courthouse and part of the contents in 1905.

When Animals Get Bewitched

Photo: Of all the animals, it was long believed that hogs were the most susceptible to bewitching. Image courtesy of Mark Peters, Poplar Spring Animal Sanctuary

In the fifth chapter of the *Gospel of Mark*, Jesus encounters a man with a legion of demons living inside him. The Bible states that the man "had his dwelling among the tombs; and no man could bind him, no, not with chains… And always, night and day, he was in the mountains, and in the tombs, crying, and cutting himself with stones…"

But when the man saw Jesus, he ran to him, begging for mercy. When Jesus spoke the demons exited the man. According to the account, the demons asked Christ to allow them to enter into a herd of swine feeding on the countryside, which Jesus authorized, and upon entering the swine, the legion of demonic hogs ran violently down the mountainside "down a steep place into the sea… and were choked in the sea…"

Though this account of possessed pigs, found also in the *Gospel of Luke*, is the only time we read of bewitched animals in the New Testament, in the early days of American and Appalachian settlement, tales of bewitched animals are too numerous to catalog.

Just about everyone knows of the tragedy of the Salem Witch Trials, but few realize that two dogs also lost their lives due to the impulsive fears of the townspeople.

Massachusetts historian Rebecca Beatrice Brooks, writes, "Since it was believed at the time that witches had animal familiars, or helpers, that they used to do their bidding, many villagers were often on the lookout for these possessed animals, which were thought to take the form of almost any creature, from cats and dogs to birds, oxes, cows or pigs."

According to Brooks, in October 1692, an afflicted Salem girl accused a neighbor's dog of trying to bewitch her. The villagers shot the dog immediately; however, after the animal's death, the local minister declared the dog to be innocent because it was reasoned that if an animal was the devil, it would be impossible to kill — thus the only way to determine if an animal was or was not bewitched would be to attempt to kill it: if it died, it was innocent, if it lived, it was guilty.

As superstitious as the pilgrims of New England were, they were rivaled by the men and women who crested the Blue Ridge and settled in what would become known as the Appalachians.

"Many of them came from lands where superstition existed and living here in the woods where so many strange things were found which they could not explain, they naturally gave a superstitious reason for them… The belief in the power of witches was prevalent in the early days. In fact, these creatures seemed to be the source of the greatest trouble to the pioneer. If the horse's mane got in a bad tangle some witch had done it. Cows would become bewitched and kick over the milk bucket. Sometimes one could churn and churn and keep on churning and the butter would not come. To break the witch's spell on the cow, they cut a small piece from the end of the cow's tail and together with a few drops of her blood and a little of her milk, put them into the hottest part of the fire; the witches could not stand the heat and so they would leave the cow in peace," wrote G.G. Williams in 1916.

Hogs would often get bewitched as well and they, too, would have their tails cut, but instead of mixing the tail with milk, they would drive a small nail through the tail and then place the severed body part into the hottest part of the fire.

According to Williams, an old German living in Appalachia had lost a large hog. He hunted far and near for her but not finding her, he went many miles away to an old man who was said to be a witch doctor. The witch doctor claimed that a witch had gotten into the hog and she had ran away. The owner was instructed to get a wisp of straw, twist it into a tight knot, put some salt over it, set it on fire and while it was burning to repeat several verses of Scripture; this would certainly scorch the witch out. The man did as he was instructed and in a few days the lost animal returned, greatly to the satisfaction of the owner and much to the credit of the witch doctor.

If a farmer went out to milk his cow and the cow did not produce an adequate supply of milk, it was believed that a neighboring witch had milked her dry. Though there was no antidote for this, the witch could be discovered by building a new pin for the cow and laying a new towel over the pin. If a woman passed by the property soon afterwards, she was the witch who had milked the cow dry.

Interestingly, even guns, stoves, spinning wheels, looms and bake ovens did not escape the peculiar power of the witch.

It is said the first glass blowers who came to this country claimed their furnaces, when they did not heat rightly, were bewitched. To break the spell, they did a most cruel thing: throwing live puppies into the fire.

Witches were said to have enjoyed playing strange pranks on people by attacking them in bizarre ways. They would sometimes catch a person out alone at night and would throw a bridle over their heads and force a bit into their mouths — changing them instantly into a horse, upon which they would mount and ride furiously all night over hills and valleys, through woods and briers until they would exhaust them.

It was claimed that cattle could even be killed by witches, who would make "witch balls", balls made of witch hair, which they would throw at the animals and kill them instantly.

One could never find where the skin had been broken on an animal killed by a witch ball; however, it was said that if the animal would be cut open, a clump of the witch ball could easily be found.

When children got sick the cause might be due to the influence of some woman, usually an old one in the neighborhood. The cure for this was to draw her picture on a paper or board and shoot it with a silver bullet. This was done in Jefferson County once, when they were about ready to shoot, some of the family went into where the accused old woman was to watch the witch fly out of her window. As the shot was fired, it being close to the house, the old lady jumped at the sudden shockwave of the gun — this was taken to mean she was guilty.

A dog howling at night certainly meant a death in the neighborhood, especially if someone were sick at the time. When any one died someone had to go and tell the bees or there would be another death in the same family within a year.

The Fearsome Fairies of the Dark Woodlands

Introducing Fairies

While modern mothers and children alike often think of Tinker Bell when they hear of fairies, Appalachian mothers a century or more ago imagined something far more sinister.

17th Century Christian Teachings Regarding Fairies

King James, in his dissertation *Daemonologie*, stated the term "faries" referred to illusory spirits (demonic entities) that prophesied to, consorted with, and transported the individuals they served; in medieval times, a witch or sorcerer who had a compact with a familiar spirit might receive these services – in essence, they were the entities witches and wizards would go to when their own powers fell short.

A popular Christian tenet for many years held that fairies were a class of demonic angels who had been cast out of heaven when Satan rebelled against God.

Given their supposed demonic origins, fairies were the subject of great fear among the highlanders of Appalachia and would often be blamed for bizarre happenings which could not be explained naturally.

A recorded Christian belief of the 17th Century cast all fairies as demons. This perspective grew more popular with the rise of Puritanism among the Reformed Church of England and quickly spread to the North American colonies, beginning in New England.

The hobgoblin, once a friendly household spirit, became classed as a wicked goblin.

Dealing with fairies was considered a form of witchcraft, and punished as such.

In William Shakespeare's *A Midsummer Night's Dream*, Oberon, king of the faeries, states that neither he nor his court fear the church bells.

Fairies in Islam

Interestingly, the belief in fairies, tiny mystical creatures which hide beneath of the cover of thick vegetation in the dark wooded areas of a forest, is not limited to European-Americans. As a matter of fact, several cultures throughout the world share some type of belief in these mystical creatures. The Persians believed in the existence of "Peri", exquisite, winged spirits renowned for their beauty. Originally from Persian and Armenian mythologies, Peris were later adopted by other cultures. They were described as mischievous beings that had been denied entry to paradise until they have completed penance for atonement.

With the spread of Islam through Persia, the Peri was integrated into Islamic folklore. They are often regarded as a kind of good jinn, while the evil ones are often identified by Persians as divs.

The belief in Peri still persist among Muslims in India as a type of spiritual creature besides the jinn, shayatin and the ghosts of the wicked.

According to the Persian exegesis of the Qur'an Tafsir al-Tabari, the peris are beautiful female spirits created by Allah.

They are still part of some folklore and accordingly they appear to humans, sometimes punishing hunters in the mountains who are disrespectful or waste resources, or even abducting young humans for their social events. Encounters with peris are held to be physical as well as psychological.

Native American's Belief in Fairies

The Europeans and Islamic world situated across the Atlantic were not the only civilizations to believe in tiny creatures hiding in the wilderness – this belief has been part of the folklore of many cultures in human history, including Ireland, Greece, the Philippines, and the Hawaiian Islands; however, the most committed people to this persuasion were by far the Native Americans — and the Cherokee in particular.

While the Holy Bible speaks about ancient "giants" who roamed the earth during the days of Noe, Native American legends speak of a race of "tiny people" who lived in wooded and rocky areas.

Often described as "hairy-faced dwarfs" in stories, petroglyph illustrations show them with horns on their head and traveling in groups of 5 to 7 per canoe.

Native legends often talk of the tiny people playing pranks on individuals, such as singing and then hiding when an inquisitive person searches for the music. It is often said that the little people love children and would take them away from bad or abusive parents or if the child was without parents and left in the woods to fend for themselves.

Other legends say the tiny people if seen by an adult human would beg them not to say anything of their existence and would reward those who kept their word by helping them and their family out in times of need. From tribe to tribe there are variations of what the tiny people's mannerisms were like, and whether they were good or evil may be different dependent upon the local tribe's passed down stories.

One of the more widely held beliefs maintained that the tiny people created distractions in order to cause mischief. They were believed to be gods by some.

One North American Native tribe believed that the tiny people lived in nearby caves. The caves were never entered for fear of disturbing the tiny people.

Though the vast majority of things believed about these "tiny people" is seen clearly as the stuff of legend by everyone today, there are a handful of evidences which seem to indicate that there could possibly be a smidgen of validity to some of these widely held stories.

An 1876 *New York Times* article describes numerous graves discovered in Tennessee that contain skeletons of Pygmies. Initially, the remains were thought to be those of children, however, later examination revealed that this is probably not the case:

"In this state [Tennessee], burying grounds have been found where the skeleton appear all to have been pygmies… it is affirmed that the skulls are found to have possessed the dentes sapientiae [Wisdom teeth] and must have belonged to persons of mature age. … two bodies that were found in the vast limestone cavern… neither of them more than four feet high: the hair seemed to be sandy or inclining to the yellow."

According to Cherokee legend, a group of tiny people known as the "Yunwi Tsunsdi'" inhabited the Appalachian Mountains. These individuals were believed to have spent much of their time drumming and dancing. It has been postulated that if there was any truth to this Cherokee belief, then the bones found in Tennessee could belong to those of the "Yunwi Tsunsdi'".

The Pigmy Tribes of the Ohio Valley, states, "One far flung theory is presented by Virgilio R. Pilapil, who asserts that the Tennessee graves did contain pygmy remains and that the pygmies arrived in ancient times from southeast Asia, where today's diminutive Aetas live."

Charms and Protections Against Fairies

Large portions of the below account have been made possible thanks to the online encyclopedia, Wikipedia's article titled, "Fairies". The below section is made available through Creative Common / Share-Alike License. Wikipedia® is a registered trademark of the Wikimedia Foundation, Inc., a non-profit organization dedicated to advancing knowledge.

With laws denouncing the celebration of fairies as a form of witchcraft and a great distrust in the tiny witches, the witch doctors, clergymen and elderly of the day provided numerous instructions on how to guard oneself against an attack from fairies:

In terms of protective charms, wearing clothing inside out, church bells, St. John's wort, and four-leaf clovers are regarded as effective.

In Canadian folklore, the most popular type of fairy protection is bread, varying from stale bread to hard tack or a slice of fresh home-made bread. Bread is associated with the home and the hearth, as well as with industry and the taming of nature, and as such, seems to be disliked by some types of fairies – not to mention the fact that Jesus stated, "I am the bread of life…"

On the other hand, in much of the Celtic tradition, baked goods are a traditional offering to the fairies, as are cream and butter.

"The prototype of food, and therefore a symbol of life, bread was one of the commonest protections against fairies. Before going out into a fairy-haunted place, it was customary to put a piece of dry bread in one's pocket," writes one commentator.

In County Wexford, Ireland, in 1882, it was reported that "if an infant is carried out after dark and a piece of bread is wrapped in its bib or dress, this will protect it from any witchcraft or evil."

While many fairies will confuse travelers on the path, the will o' the wisp can be avoided by not following it.

Certain locations, known to be haunts of fairies, are to be avoided; C. S. Lewis reported hearing of a cottage more feared for its reported fairies than its reported ghost.

In particular, digging in fairy hills was unwise.

Paths that the fairies travel are also wise to avoid. Home-owners have knocked corners from houses because the corner blocked the fairy path, and cottages have been built with the front and back doors in line, so that the owners could, in need, leave them both open and let the fairies troop through all night.

Locations such as fairy forts were left undisturbed; even cutting brush on fairy forts was reputed to be the death of those who performed the act.

Fairy trees, such as thorn trees, were dangerous to chop down; one such tree was left alone in Scotland, though it prevented a road being widened for seventy years.

In Scotland, fairies were often mischievous and to be feared. No one dared to set foot in the mill or kiln at night, as it was known that the fairies brought their corn to be milled after dark. So long as the locals believed this, the miller could sleep secure in the knowledge that his stores were not being robbed. John Fraser, the miller of Whitehill, claimed to have hidden and watched the fairies trying unsuccessfully to work the mill. He said he decided to come out of hiding and help them, upon which one of the fairy women gave him a gowpen (double handful of meal) and told him to put it in his empty girnal (store), saying that the store would remain full for a long time, no matter how much he took out.

It is also believed that to know the name of a particular fairy could summon it to you and force it to do your bidding.

Before the advent of modern medicine, many physiological conditions were untreatable and when children were born with abnormalities, it was common to blame the fairies.

Deadly Fairy Games: The Changeling

Of all the superstitions held by our ancient ancestors of Europe, it's hard to imagine any which has claimed the number of innocent lives as much as the belief in changelings.

A changeling was believed to have been a creature the fairies had left in place for a human child they had stolen – though the child's features and physical appearance may have been unchanged, it was commonly believed that the child itself had been taken and living inside the shell of what was once the child was a fraudulent counterfeit.

A child was especially thought to have become a changeling when he or she suddenly and without any explanation became sick or developed an unexplained disease, disorder, or developmental disability.

It would be impossible to detail the countless number of changeling stories said to have occurred over the centuries, but it is believed that thousands of children may have died due to their parents mistaking them to have been a changeling.

D. L. Ashliman, Professor Emeritus of German at the University of Pittsburgh, is an American folklorist and generally considered to be a leading expert on folklore and fairytales.

Asliman translated an 1816 German account of a supposed changeling, *A Changeling is Beaten with a Switch*, which goes along the following:

According to Asliman's translation, in 1580, near Breslau, a new mother was working to harvest a large crop of hay one summer. The woman, who had barely had a week to recover from the birth of her child, took the baby and placed it on a small clump of grass, and left it alone while she helped with the haymaking.

After she had worked a long time, she returned to the newborn infant and upon simply looking at it, she began to cry and scream aloud – the child was not hers but had become a changeling.

As the story goes, the baby sucked the milk from her "so greedily and howled in such an inhuman manner that it was nothing like the child she knew."

She took the baby home and after several days of the child not acting like the babe she knew, she told her story to the nobleman who told her, "If you think that this is not your child, then do this one thing. Take it out to the meadow where you left your previous child and beat it hard with a switch. Then you will witness a miracle."

As the story concludes, the woman followed the nobleman's advice and went out and beat the child with a switch until it began screaming very loudly. Then the Devil brought back her stolen child, saying: "There, you have it!" And with that he took his own child away.

It was believed that one's baby could be returned by the fairies by doing a number of different things; a popular practice involved confusing the changeling by cooking or brewing in eggshells – this nonsense would force the changeling to speak, thus revealing its true age.

More violent levels included attempting to trying to burn the changeling in the oven as well as hitting or whipping the changeling, all of which would immediately summon the changeling's parents or the devil who would then be ready to trade back the human baby for the changeling.

As difficult as this belief in changelings may be to believe in modern society, these were not some fringe notions held by a wily few a handful of centuries ago, but shared and even propagated by many of the leading minds of the hour.

William R. Albury, PhD, is adjunct professor of history in the School of Humanities at the University of New England, Armidale, Australia, and he writes, "The idea of the changeling draws on the ancient folk belief that an abnormal child was not the real child of its putative parents, but a spirit, such as an elf, fairy, or goblin, left in the real child's stead. Having been abducted from the parents, the true child was raised amongst its supernatural abductors, while the otherworldly child remained.

Consistent with the more severe manifestations of autism, most changelings lacked typical social behavior. Refraining from talk or laughter, they would cry incessantly, remain silent, or seem to find enjoyment at someone else's distress. On rare occasions, a changeling might unexpectedly utter a word or two, giving the impression that the creature obstinately refused to speak despite an ability to do so.

"Often changelings were described as physically grotesque, but some of them, like some autistic individuals, were said to be of normal appearance and show exceptional ability in a single area such as music or concentrated work (MacCulloch). A well-known historical example of a reputed changeling is the 12-year-old Saxon boy to whom Martin Luther referred in a biblical commentary of 1535 and a discussion with his associates in 1540.

"As the child was said to be able to do nothing but eat and excrete, Luther regarded it as a mass of flesh animated not by a human soul but by a devil. The situation, he believed, was one in which the devil had acted "to remove a child completely and put himself into the cradle in place of the stolen child" (Miles 30-31).

Suspected changelings were thrown into water, beaten severely, left unfed in fields or forests or burned in hot stoves – all in hopes of the parents getting their original baby back.

However, Pittsburgh's Professor Asliman, who is one of the world's leading authorities on European superstitions, postulates that these ghastly actions may not have been simply the unwitting work of innocent and ignorant parents, but rather an acceptable excuse for legal and socially acceptable infanticide.

"There is ample evidence that these legendary accounts do not misrepresent or exaggerate the actual abuse of suspected changelings…. A peasant family's very subsistence frequently depended upon the productive labor of each member, and it was enormously difficult to provide for a person who was a permanent drain on the family's scarce resources. The fact that the changelings' ravenous appetite is so frequently mentioned indicates that the parents of these unfortunate children saw in their continuing existence a threat to the sustenance of the entire family. Changeling tales support other historical evidence in suggesting that infanticide was not infrequently the solution selected," writes Asliman.

Foxfire: Fairy Fire

The enchanting forests located just our doors in the Appalachian hillsides are dark and mystical, hiding an untold number of mysterious features never to be known by humans, in fact, the vast majority of nature's secrets are seldom even spotted by man's weak eyes.

Planet earth is filled with natural wonders capable of leaving the viewer both astonied and inspired – but even when one considers the millions of incredible phenomenon nature showcases each day, it's hard to imagine anything more incredible, frightening and as mystifying as a natural event that goes by one of two names: "foxfire" or "fairy fire".

To the unsuspecting observer, stumbling upon a foxfire can be an alarming sight in the blackness of night, deep in the dense forests of a darkened underworld, but to the student of science, the sight of a fairy fire glowing atop a log is true magic.

At its core, fairy fires are a bioluminescence light created by some species of fungi present in decaying wood. Emitting a bluish-green glow due to a chemical reaction taking place inside the fungi's enzyme, a foxfire's light can on a few rare occasions be bright enough to read by.

Scientists have speculated that the purpose of the light is to attract insects that will spread spores, further growing the fungi. Others have hypothesized that the light serves as a warning to hungry animals, as bright colors are often exhibited by poisonous or unpalatable plants to many animals in the forest.

The oldest recorded documentation of foxfire is from 382 B.C., by Aristotle, whose notes refer to a light that, unlike fire, was cold to the touch. The Roman thinker Pliny the Elder also mentioned glowing wood in olive groves.

Foxfire was used to illuminate the needles on the barometer and the compass of early submarines.

Throughout the early days of mining, foxfires were often spotted glowing from wooden support beams inside mines.

In addition to serving as the title to a series of handy books about Appalachian culture from the last half-century, foxfire has also made an appearance in a Smurfs episode. In the episode, "The Smurf who couldn't say no", Pushover Smurf was instructed to gather foxfire from a marsh for a firefly festival.

It is interesting to note that "fireflies" aka "lightning bugs", glow due to the same substance that makes foxfire shine, a naturally occurring chemical known as luciferin.

Though science has sufficiently explained "fairy fire" for most people, roughly a century ago, it was commonly believed that "flame wood", as it was also known, served as lanterns for fairies who were traveling at nighttime.

Death Circles: Fairy Rings

Walking outside of one's house in the early morning of the day, only to

Photo: "Fairy Rings", courtesy of Sarah Kirby, Wythe Co., Virginia

be greeted by the unexpected sight of a symmetrical circle of mushrooms that appeared overnight can be a hair-raising experience to say the least.

Surprisingly, this phenomena is actually far more common than one might think and is the subject of mountain lore dating back ages.

Known as "Fairy Rings" and "Elf Circles", these circular groupings of mushrooms have grown to reach a diameter of roughly half a mile and one in Belfort, France, is believed to be over 700 years old.

The Science Behind Fairy Rings

Though they are formed mainly in forested areas, they sometimes appear in grassy places and are made when mycelium of a fungus growing in the ground absorbs nutrients. This breaks down larger molecules in the soil into smaller molecules that are then absorbed through the walls of the hyphae near their growing tips. The mycelium will move outward from the center, and when the nutrients in the center are exhausted, the center dies, thereby forming a living ring, from which the fairy ring arises.

Rings of Sorcery

Appalachian, as well as ancient folklore is riddled with mentions of fairy rings, which are also known as "sorcerers' rings" in France and "witches' rings" in German tradition, all of which are believed to appear on the sites of where witches had danced the previous night – Western European traditions, including English, Scandinavian and Celtic, claimed that fairy rings are the result of elves or fairies dancing.

Early Appalachian settlers believed that fairy rings were dangerous places that should be avoided, stating that trespassing into the forbidden ring could end in great curses upon the encroacher.

Welch tradition teaches that fairies force morals into the ring in hopes of dancing with them, but once the person steps foot inside the ring, the individual's life will be cut premature with exhaustion, death, or madness.

Teardrops of the Fairies: Virginia's Fairy Crosses

Photo: Fairy Crosses Courtesy of Virginia State Parks

Appalachia's early Cherokee inhabitants believed they shared the land with a tiny race of people they described as having hairy faces and living in wooded and rocky areas of the mountains.

Native legends often speak of the tiny people playing pranks on individuals, such as singing and then hiding when an inquisitive person searches for the music. It was often said that the little people loved children and would take them away from bad or abusive parents.

With Scottish and Irish folklore including tales of fairies, changelings and many similar mythical beliefs, the original European settlers who first entered Virginia's mountains were willing candidates to receive the Native's belief and even added their own superstitions to those long held by the Cherokee.

As the foothills of the Blue Ridge Mountains were explored, various individuals happened upon mysterious cross shaped rocks, often no larger than one's smallest fingernail. The rocks included what appeared to be perfect cutouts of both Roman crosses (traditional t-shape) as well as St. Andrews' crosses (X-shaped).

In an effort to explain the rocks' origins, legends throughout the mountainside developed stating that long ago the fairies who inhabited the area received word detailing the dreadful agonies Christ suffered in his crucifixion. The news caused the fairies to weep and as their tears fell to the ground, they crystalized into little stone crosses.

Often the words of Jesus quoted in Luke 19.40 have been included with tales of the Fairy Stones, "I tell you that, if these should hold their peace, the stones would immediately cry out."

Scientists say the stones are comprised of iron, aluminum and silicate.

According to Virginia State Park officials, the staurolite crystals were formed thanks to a precise combination of heat and pressure provided by the folding and crumpling of the earth's crust during the formation of the Appalachian Mountains.

In an effort to preserve the site where these mysterious stone crosses were first discovered, the Commonwealth of Virginia created Fairy Stone State Park in 1936, one of the original six state parks created that year.

The park's land was donated by Junius B. Fishburn, former owner of the Roanoke Times.

As the 4,741-acre park celebrates its 82nd year of operation, attractions include cabins, a campground, group camping, an equestrian campground, a conference center, hiking trails, lake swimming, rowboats, canoes, paddle boats, kayaks, picnicking and two playgrounds, including one in the water.

Visitors may also hunt for "Fairy Stones", as "a small number may be taken for personal use."

**

In 1909, G.O. Stovall published the following article in Harper's Weekly, detailing Virginia's Mysterious Fairy Stones:

Fairy Stones: The Ultimate Good Luck Charm

Near the point where the Blue Ridge and the Allegheny mountains unite, north of Patrick County, Virginia, lie the Meadows of Dan. It is not far from this remarkable plateau on the side of the Bull Mountain, a spur of the Blue Ridge, that fairy stones are found. They are little natural crosses... and geologists assert that they have never been found elsewhere.

These stones, which range in size from one fourth to one ounce, are all in the form of crosses. Some are Roman, some Maltese, and some St. Andrews.

Frequently they are joined together making a remarkable combination. No two are exactly alike. Some are as tiny as a pin, others weigh as much as an ounce and a half. They also vary in color, the handsomest are a rich maroon with the lustre of highly polished onyx, others are amber and porphyry brown, while the commonest are rough and resemble ordinary bits of rock. Some of these stones which were analyzed contained titanite, tourmaline, garnet, and steatite, being the principal material.

Geologists say they are crystals, but fail to explain why they belong exclusively to this spot.

Virginia's Pilgrims Crystals, resembling these, have been discovered but the perfect cross or fairy stone has been nowhere else found, not even in any other part of Patrick County.

A few years ago these stones were first brought to notice by a mineralogist while making a tour on horseback through this mountainous region. Until then they were known only to the people of that section of the State...

The snake hunter, moonshiner, and the ginseng gatherer, constitute the people of that wild and rugged country, they who defy the law and glory in the fastness and security of their abode. To this class, the fairy stone is a thing of superstitious adoration. They believe that evil in all forms is averted if they wear one of these stones about their neck and to lose it signifies disaster.

No distance is too great and no height nor depth so inaccessible as to prevent these mountain pilgrims from the possession of a fairy stone.

For a century this superstition has existed and has descended from one generation to another and today they will tell you with a childlike faith of the marvelous power of these little crosses.

A Mountain Superstition

You may see the broad breasted, tawny haired moonshiner with his free swinging gait, making his way to the spot. An earnest look is in his blue eyes and the spring of a strong motive in his stride. He reaches the vicinity in which the stones are found.

He looks about, stamps the earth here and there, then he probably will unsheath a big horn handled knife and begin digging, as he crouches low to the earth – he has found the mother stone and a Roman cross strikes against his blade, but that is not what he is looking for; he wants a Maltese cross that he considers blesses him with success in his business, helps him to evade the revenue officers who are the only disturbers from the outer world who hunt him down, it will give him the power of concealment.

His still, in the crevice of the rocks, will be safe, so long as the little stone cross presses against his breast and with this faith, he continues his search.

He digs and gouges in the earth with his big strong hands until he finds what he is seeking. He picks from a fissure, a bit of dirt crusted rock, with the point of his knife he scrapes the grit and earth from around it. His eyes dance, his broad mouth breaks into a smile. It is a Maltese cross. He takes a cord from his pocket, winds it about the arms of the cross with clumsy security, then ties it around his neck.

With the consciousness of absolute power, he straightens himself as much as to say, "Now I defy the law," and with alert swiftness, turns his face towards the pinnacles of Dan that lie many miles beyond the moonshiner's paradise – they are called on account of their inaccessibility.

These two immense natural pyramids rise to a level with the surrounding mountains around which the river Dan encircles, running around each pinnacle, one at a time.

From all sections of Patrick County and far beyond, the people make pilgrimages to the fairy stone shrine. In contrast to the mountain Hercules, you may see a slender pallid faced woman picking her way down a cragged height, bearing in her arms her sick child. She does not consider the distance or difficulties that lie in her path, but taking up her babe, she leaves her hut and goes her way, believing that if she can but place upon the breast of her child a Roman cross, fresh with the mould and grit from the bed of the shrine, the babe will be healed.

A Charm for Love

You may also see a young ginseng gatherer looking like some flower of the mountain gorge, with her yellow hair blowing against the fresh cool breeze and her blue homespun gown hugging tight her straight rounded limbs. She is making her way there also, but she tells nobody what kind of a cross she seeks. But watch and you will see she looks until a little double Maltese is found, which she presses to her lips, then ties it on a string and suspends it around her neck.

"Now I ain'ter skeerin' ov no gal in all ov Patrick's County. Tibe Bleeks is mine sure. Nancy and Peg and all ov the res' ain'ter goi'n to skeer me."

Jealousy and doubt are exorcised as the rough little twin crosses grate against her breast and on she goes with this assurance giving strength to her waning hope.

And so these mountain folk come and go, just as they have done for more than a century – some on oxen, some on donkeys, but the greater number on foot.

The origins of Fairy Stones

There are many legends as to the origin of these stones. The one generally accepted and from which their name – "fairy stones" – is derived, is that when Christ was crucified on Calvary, courier fairies and brownies from that part of the world carried the message to that section, where they at once began making these crosses as mementoes of the event, but there are many who accept the belief that when the native Indians inhabited the country, these crosses were miraculously showered upon them as a means of turning them from their bloodthirsty and idolatrous ways.

Powhatan Bouldin, a direct descendant of Pocahontas, and one of the most distinguished and scholarly men of Virginia has in his possession several exquisite arrowheads beautifully carved from rock crystal which together with similar relics he found in the meadows near the head waters of Smith River, only a short distance from Bull Mountain, where the fairy stones abound.

The superstition is not confined to the moonshiner and snake hunter element now. It is spreading over all sections of Virginia and other States as well. Many prominent men wear them secretly as a mascot, while others wear them handsomely mounted as watch charms, scarf pins, cuff buttons, and other ornaments.

Ex-President Cleveland was presented with one of these previously to receiving his second nomination.

It is said that the natives in that part of Patrick County who have for generations given reverence to these stones for their marvelous powers resent the idea of their circulation as "luck stones" or ornaments.

The Mystical Trees of Appalachia

Despite being branded as 'wild and wonderful,' the sad reality is that Appalachia's present-day forests are but a frail shell of what they were only a handful of centuries ago.

Once upon a time, not too long ago, the unmolested forests of America's eastern mountains would have been unrecognizable to its modern-day inhabitants. They were far darker than we know them as today and were home to an incredible number of species whose days have long since passed: the multi-color Carolina Parakeet, the Eastern Bison and the preying Eastern Mountain Lion (the fourth largest cat on the planet), all called the mountains of Southern Appalachia home before many of our ancestors arrived.

Indeed, the modern forests of home are almost unrecognizable compared to the majestic, dense and dark foggy woodland that greeted the first white settlers only a handful of centuries ago.

Though the loss of the forest's original inhabitants has been great, the greatest loss in these forests may possibly have been the forests themselves.

One of the earliest men to write about the region's ancient forests was a young surveyor by the name of George Washington.

On November 4, 1770, while plotting the Kanawha River, he wrote in his journal, "Just as we came to the hills, we met with a Sycamore... of a most extraordinary size, it measuring three feet from the ground, forty-five feet round, lacking two inches; and not fifty yards from it was another, thirty-one feet round."

Bill Grafton, president of the West Virginia Native Plant Society stated, "In Pre-Colonial times, the 15 million acres of West Virginia were almost entirely forested."

The trees, centuries-old colossal mammoths, towered proudly over the Appalachia — standing like skyscrapers of the ancient world, reigning for thousands of years over the majestic and unconquerable land. Older than the Mayflower, many of the region's white oak and hemlock trees were more than half-a-millennium old – an unimaginable spectacle for the European colonists who first laid eyes on the trees.

Because of these truths, it should come as no surprise that for the early white inhabitants of Appalachia, the trees around them often possessed a mystical power.

Bottle Trees

If you're a child of the American Southland or Appalachia, odds are you have come across "bottle trees" at some time or another in your life – typically a bare tree which may have dozens of bottles covering dead limbs and branches. In other instances, the bottles would be attached to trees via string, tied around the branches.

In more recent decades, this bizarre practice has become largely decorative; however, less than a century ago, the act of placing bottles over tree branches or tying them to limbs was a spiritual act rooted in African voodoo and witchcraft.

According to historians, "Bottle Trees" came to the Old South from Africa with the slave trade. Bottle trees were an African tradition, passed down from early Arabian traders. They believed that the bottles trapped the evil spirits until the rising morning sun could destroy them. The use of blue bottles is linked to the "haint blue" spirit specifically.

These bottles would often be tied to trees near a crossroad or at a prominent location in order to capture any spirits which may be traveling.

Though the superstition has all but been lost in recent years, the practice is actually rising in popularity throughout the nation as a popular garden decoration.

Rag Trees

Much like bottle trees, another superstitious practice regarding trees involved tying rags around the branches.

Known as "patting", the observer of this practice takes the filthy rags from a sick or dying person and ties them to a tree – a thorny one if possible.

According to superstition, if the person's disease or sickness is the result of some spiritual activity, the tree will catch their disease and thereby alleviate the afflicted person of their ailment.

Leaving an Apple for the Devil

Throughout the mountains of Appalachia, only a century ago, it was customary to leave a ripe apple hanging on the tree following each harvest. This apple was left for the devil to enjoy, in order to ensure he would continue on his journey and not become angry with the inhabitants of the house for not leaving him food.

Under a Pine Tree, Hearing Angels Sing

It was also held that if an individual sat under a pine tree on Christmas Day, they might be able to catch a glimpse of angels singing, but word of caution to the soul desirous of doing this – hearing them sing would signify that the listener would be on their way to heaven before the next Christmas.

Don't Plant a Cedar Tree

In January 1969, Historian Wylene P. Dial noted why there were so few cedar trees in Lincoln County, West Virginia: "It seems to stem from the conviction held by a number of people that if someone plants a cedar he will die when it grows large enough to shade his coffin."

When Chilly Death Comes to Visit

Photo: Funeral procession of Devil Anse Hatfield. 1921.

Death Comes in Threes
My grandfather died, then my uncle suddenly passed away within no more than two weeks time, and immediately, a feeling of anxiety swept over the mountains of southern West Virginia as our entire family began eyeing each other – and some themselves – as we awaited the impending third death which seemed inevitable.

Dating back to my boyhood, when I remember attending my first "wake" all the way up to this past week, I've heard it said a countless number of times throughout the mountains of Appalachia — "They come in threes!"

Fortunately for our family, the unthinkable happened and we were spared from the third funeral – perhaps someone took the effort to invite the bees to my uncle's funeral.

While I'll be the first to admit that those of us who grew up in the mountains of Appalachia are privy to some pretty wild superstitions, particularly when it comes to death, i.e., birds singing outside one's window at nighttime means a death is coming... as does rocking an empty rocking chair; however, the "death comes in threes" notion is one that I tend to believe – ever the more so as I grow older.

I cannot count how many times I've seen this take place with my own eyes — Let's not forget about the time Michael Jackson, Ed McMahon and Farrah Fawcett all died in the same week.

But why do so many people believe this and what are the origins of this mysterious belief?

Like a countless number of other Appalachian beliefs and superstitions, the notion of people dying off in threes can be traced back across the Atlantic to our European ancestors, who, thanks to an unshakable belief in the Trinity, began to see everything broken into sections of threes — tragedies, births, etc.

While there remains considerable debate as to whether folks in a community or family actually do pass away in threes, the reality is that if you're in Appalachia, you simply won't have to go too far to find someone who believes this — perhaps even myself!

Three: The Number of Bad Luck

Though the Chinese have long considered three to be a lucky number, for Americans and their European counterparts three has often been synonymous with bad luck, except of course when we say, "The third time's a charm!"

During the twentieth century, it was long considered to be an unlucky thing to be the third person in a group to light a cigarette from the same match or lighter. It is believed that this superstition originated among soldiers in the trenches of the World War I when a sniper might see the first light, take aim on the second and fire on the third.

Dying on a Feather Bed

The following article was written by Dr. Henry R. Ford, in the Meyer Brothers Druggist, in 1907.

"If you ever should practice medicine," said the doctor, "one day you will appreciate what it means to a country doctor to ride up to a house where he has a patient whose prognosis is doubtful and see the feather bed and the bed clothes all out on the fence."

My early experience soon taught me that this was a pretty sure sign of death and one time during the second year of my practice, I caused quite a commotion in a certain neighborhood by reporting one of the prominent men dead, when he was not!

I had given him up any way, in my own mind, and when I reached the hill overlooking my patient's farm and saw the bedding out on the fence and a group of neighbors in the yard, I took it for granted that he was dead and turned my horse around and started back.

On my way I met several of the neighbors who asked how Abe Cole was and I made them all an answer that he was dead. When I arrived home, I told my wife that Abe Cole had died.

One of the editors got a hold of it and announced that Abraham Cole, one of the most prominent farmers of Jasper Township had died.

Imagine my surprise a few days later when passing through Abe Cole's neighborhood to learn that he was sitting up and would be out in a short time and had sworn vengeance on the editor and doctor for reporting him dead!

I succeeded in pacifying him, however, and even collected my bill. But it taught me a lesson which I have never forgotten.

This reminds me of a superstition which may be of interest to you:

When a person dies on a feather bed, if his spirit goes to wear a crown in the better land, there will be found in the bed a small crown formed of the feathers; However, if his future abode is to be in the other place, no crown will be found. I have heard people solemnly declare that they had seen these crowns.

Pushing a Corpse Feet First

Coroners and individuals who are training to serve in the funeral industry learn very early on of the importance of transporting the deceased feet first. There are a number of practical reasons this is the case; the head end of a body bag is where the zipper begins, which means a worker only needs to unzip a small portion to identify the face.

Also, the torso and upper body is the heavier section of an individual, which means that the feet-first method ensures the person pushing a stretcher is steering from the heavier end and thus has greater control of the body and cart.

In addition to practicality, however, there are even weightier symbolisms attached to the feet first method:

For starters, the direction our feet are pointed in reveal the direction our body is traveling – this is true when we walk, sit in a car or even do something like riding a sled down a hill in wintertime.

Because of this reality, pushing a corpse headfirst is thought to place the body in a very unnatural state and has been whispered to upset the spirit of the deceased.

During the early years of our ancestors settling the Appalachians, many believed that if a corpse was taken out of a home head first, the deceased would be able to look back and beckon someone from the home to accompany them in death.

Stopping Clocks

I was a broken-hearted teenage boy one spring afternoon in early April, in what seems on one hand like only yesterday, but on the other, more like a century ago.

My grandfather, best friend and one person whom I desired to be more like than anyone else I knew, died after a prolonged illness.

A week earlier, he had been unable to rest comfortably in his bedroom, and so I held back tears as I assisted my father and uncles in moving him down the hall into a guest bedroom where caring for him would be easier for the family and there would be more room to assist him — sadly, he would never again leave that room alive.

In a matter of days we watched what I thought to be the strongest and toughest man to ever live waste away to nothing more than a gasping and broken bag of flesh. And then at last, the inevitable came: my grandfather died early one spring morning.

Frozen, I sat stoic as aunts cried, uncles left the room and a devastated family began to face the heartbreaking realization that grandpa was gone.

In what seemed to me to be so bizarre and out of place, I watched as my mourning grandmother stood to her feet, walked over to the grandfather clock that had gone completely unnoticed over the previous week and stopped its pendulum.

Years later, out of respect for her and in memory of that terrible hour, that aged grandfather clock has stood silent. Frozen at 7:05 a.m.

But why? Why did she do this?

I have often wondered about this to my self and though she has been gone for many years, the oddity of that day still puzzles me.

One day, curiosity got the better of me and I began combing the Internet for clues as to why my grandmother did this and to my surprise, it seems that my story is not too different than many other individuals.

The practice of stopping a clock following the death of a loved one is actually quite prevalent throughout America's Southland and mountain communities.

One online writer states, "In Victorian times, when someone died in the house and there was a clock in the room, you had to stop the clock at the death hour or the family of the household would have bad luck. Its origin seems to emanate from Germany and Great Britain. They believed that when a person died, time stood still for them and a new period of existence started without time. To permit time to continue was to invite the spirit of the deceased to remain and haunt unendingly. Stopping time was a way to allow the deceased to move on."

Interestingly, even the bells that were once rung at funerals are strangely and loosely connected to this belief: Bells are connected to clocks as their mechanics are similar and the stately clocks of old all contained bells which signified the hour.

By ringing bells at funerals, the family was signify a new time period had begun for the deceased.

It wasn't just superstition, however, that led many family members to stop the clocks following the death of a loved one. It was also done in order to provide a time of death for the local coroner.

As you can imagine, there are countless other mountain superstition concerning death.

Covering Mirrors

In addition to stopping clocks, a similar custom requires the living to cover all the mirrors in a home following the death of a loved one. There is debate as to why this is done, as some argue it is so that mourners do not have to see how they look when they are in mourning and can then feel free to mourn peacefully.

Others, however, argue that mirrors are covered to "allow the spirit of the newly deceased person to cross over into their new life successfully and to keep them from getting trapped in this life.

It was once believed if the soul of the newly departed saw their reflection in the mirror, they would become trapped and not be able to leave and begin their afterlife. This might cause the spirit to stay and haunt all who remain in this world.

Another superstition stated that the person who would first see their reflection in the mirror after the spirit of the deceased saw theirs would be the next person to die. Mirrors were covered so no one would see their reflection. Typically, mirrors remained covered until the day after the funeral, when they could again be uncovered.

Telling the Bees

Bees are critically important to the circle of life we enjoy in the rural hills of Appalachia. Without them, we would struggle to have our crops pollinated and enjoy the sweet taste of honey. So important they are to our daily lives, the United States Department of Agriculture estimates that one out of every three bites of food we take is derived from plants pollinated by bees.

Though the chemicals used in modern farming have in many ways contributed to declining bee populations, our ancestors recognized the critical importance bees played and honored them accordingly.

So reverenced were bees, in fact, that in Europe as well as America's mountains, for centuries, the people practiced a custom in which they would notify bees of important life events in their keeper's lives, such as births, marriages, or departures and returns in the household.

It was believed that if this custom was omitted or forgotten and the bees were not notified, the keeper would face a penalty, such as the bees leaving their hive, stopping the production of honey, or dying.

***

In 1899, Margaret Morley published the book, "The Honey-Makers". In this book, she devoted a chapter to the customs and superstitions related to honey bees and below is her account of the practice known as "telling the bees":

The bees must still be told of a death in the family in many parts of Europe and in certain out of the way places in our own country, where in earlier days the custom was general.

In England the custom of telling the bees is still general in the rural districts. Not long since, a woman in Suffolk, when asked if she had told the bees of the death of a relative, immediately replied, "Oh yes, when my aunt died I told every skep [hive] myself and put them into mourning...

In the Carolina mountains of the United States the people still tell the bees of a death in the family, as one of the mountaineers recently described it, "You knock on each hive and say, "*Lucy* is dead."

The Funeral Fire

For several nights after the interment of a Chippewa, a fire is kept burning upon the grave. This fire is lit in the evening and carefully supplied with small sticks of dry wood to keep up a bright but small fire. It is kept burning for several hours, generally until the usual hour of retiring to rest and then suffered to go out.

The fire is renewed for four nights and sometimes for longer. The person who performs this pious office is generally a near relative of the deceased or one who has been long intimate with him.

The following tale is related as showing the origin of the custom:

A small war party of Chippewas encountered their enemies upon an open plain where a severe battle was fought. Their leader was a brave and distinguished warrior, but he never acted with greater bravery or more distinguished himself by personal prowess than on this occasion. After turning the tide of battle against his enemies, while shouting for victory, he received an arrow in his breast and fell upon the plain.

No warrior thus killed is ever buried and according to ancient custom the chief was placed in a sitting posture upon the field, his back supported by a tree and his face turned towards the direction in which his enemies had fled. His headdress and equipment were accurately adjusted as if he were living and his bow leaned against his shoulder. In this posture, his companions left him.

That he was dead appeared evident to all, but a strange thing had happened. Although deprived of speech and motion, the chief heard distinctly all that was said by his friends. He heard them lament his death without having the power to contradict it and he felt their touch as they adjusted his posture without having the power to reciprocate it. His anguish when he felt himself thus abandoned was extreme and his wish to follow his friends on their return home so completely filled his mind as he saw them one after another take leave of him and depart that with a terrible effort, he arose and followed them.

His form, however, was invisible to them and this aroused in him surprise, disappointment, and rage, which by turns took possession of him.

He followed their track with great diligence.

Wherever they went, he went, when they walked he walked, when they ran, he ran, when they encamped, he stopped with them, when they slept, he slept, when they awoke, he awoke.

In short, he mingled in all their labours and toils, but he was excluded from all their sources of refreshment, except that of sleeping and from the pleasures of participating in their conversation, for all that he said received no notice.

"Is it possible," he cried, "that you do not see me, that you do not hear me, that you do not understand me?"

"Will you suffer me to bleed to death without offering to stanch my wounds? Will you permit me to starve while you eat around me? Have those whom I have so often led to war so soon forgotten me? Is there no one who recollects me or who will offer me a morsel of food in my distress?"

Thus he continued to upbraid his friends at every stage of the journey, but no one seemed to hear his words. If his voice was heard at all, it was mistaken for the rustling of the leaves in the wind.

At length, the returning party reached their village and their women and children came out, according to custom, to welcome their return and proclaim their praises.

"Kumaudjeewug! Kumaudjeewug! Kumaudjeewug!"

"They have met fought and conquered!" was shouted by every mouth and the words resounded through the most distant parts of the village.

Those who had lost friends came eagerly to inquire their fate and to know whether they had died like men. The aged father consoled himself for the loss of his son, with the reflection that he had fallen manfully and the widow half forgot her sorrow amid the praises that were uttered of the bravery of her husband.

The hearts of the youths glowed with martial ardour as they heard these flattering praises and the children joined in the shouts of which they scarcely knew the meaning. Amidst all this uproar and bustle no one seemed conscious of the presence of the warrior chief.

He heard many inquiries made respecting his fate. He heard his companions tell how he had fought, conquered, and fallen, pierced by an arrow through his breast and how he had been left behind among the slain on the field of battle.

"It is not true," declared the angry chief, "that I was killed and left upon the field, I am here. I live! I move! See me! Touch me!"

"I shall again raise my spear in battle and take my place in the feast."

Nobody, however, seemed conscious of his presence and his voice was mistaken for the whispering of the wind.

He now walked to his own lodge and there he found his wife, tearing her hair and lamenting over his fate. He endeavored to undeceive her, but she, like the others, appeared to be insensible of his presence and not to hear his voice.

She sat in a despairing manner with her head reclining on her hands. The chief asked her to bind up his wounds, but she made no reply. He placed his mouth close to her ear and shouted, "I am hungry, give me some food."

The wife thought she heard a buzzing in her ear and remarked it to one who sat by.

The enraged husband now summoning all his strength struck her a blow on the forehead. His wife raised her hand to her head and said to her friend, "I feel a slight shooting pain in my head."

Foiled thus in every attempt to make himself known, the warrior chief began to reflect upon what he had heard in his youth, to the effect that the spirit was sometimes permitted to leave the body and wander about. He concluded that possibly his body might have remained upon the field of battle, while his spirit only accompanied his returning friends. He determined to return to the field, although it was four days journey away.

He accordingly set out upon his way.

For three days he pursued his way without meeting anything uncommon, but on the fourth towards evening as he came to the skirts of the battlefield, he saw a fire in the path before him.

He walked to one side to avoid stepping into it, but the fire also changed its position and was still before him. He then went in another direction, but the mysterious fire still crossed his path and seemed to bar his entrance to the scene of the conflict. In short, whichever way he took, the fire was still before him – no expedient seemed to avail him.

"Thou demon!" he exclaimed at length, "why dost thou bar my approach to the field of battle?"

"Knowest thou not that I am a spirit also and that I seek again to enter my body? Dost thou presume that I shall return without effecting my object? Know that I have never been defeated by the enemies of my nation and will not be defeated by thee."

He then made a sudden effort and jumped through the flame.

No sooner had he done so than he found himself sitting on the ground with his back supported by a tree, his bow leaning against his shoulder, all his warlike dress and arms upon his body, just as they had been left by his friends on the day of battle.

Looking up, he beheld a large war eagle sitting in the tree above his head. He immediately recognized this bird to be the same as he had once dreamt of in his youth, the one he had chosen as his guardian spirit. This eagle had carefully watched his body and prevented other ravenous birds from touching it. The chief got up and stood upon his feet, but he felt himself weak and much exhausted.

The blood upon his wound had stanched itself and he now bound it up. He possessed a knowledge of such roots as have healing properties and these he carefully sought in the woods. Having found some, he pounded some of them between stones and applied them externally. Others he chewed and swallowed.

In a short time he found himself so much recovered as to be able to commence his journey, but he suffered greatly from hunger – not seeing any large animals that he might kill.

However, he succeeded in killing some small birds with his bow and arrow and these he roasted before a fire at night. In this way he sustained himself until he came to a river that separated his wife and friends from him. He stood upon the bank and gave that peculiar whoop which is a signal of the return of a friend.

The sound was immediately heard and a canoe was dispatched to bring him over and in a short time amidst the shouts of his friends and relations who thronged from every side to see the arrival the warrior chief was landed.

When the first wild bursts of wonder and joy had subsided and some degree of quiet had been restored to the village, he related to his people the account of his adventures.

He concluded his narrative by telling them that it is pleasing to the spirit of a deceased person to have a fire built upon the grave for four nights after his burial – that it is four days journey to the land appointed for the residence of the spirits... that in its journey thither, the spirit stands in need of a fire every night, at the place of its encampment and that if the friends kindle this fire upon the spot where the body is laid, the spirit has the benefit of its light and warmth on its path, while if the friends neglect to do this, the spirit is subjected to the irksome task of making its own fire each night.

Old Time Appalachian Tradition & Superstitions in Child Birth

Giving birth is an incredible milestone and platinum moment in any family's story – but at the same time, it is serious business and subjects a woman to extreme pain and dangers that are seldom equaled. Combining these two realities together creates the perfect conditions for unique rituals, traditions and superstitions, and in the hills of Appalachia, the place I proudly claim as home, things are no different.

Nearly a half century ago, my mother, at my grandmother's insistence, "flipped me", doused urine into my ear, fed me catnip and probably did a hundred other things folks outside of the mountains would be aghast to hear – finding them to be strange at best, and abuse at worst.

Fortunately, I survived and in some strange way, many years later, I am very proud of this rich mountain heritage that began long before my eyes ever beheld the light of day.

My great-great-grandmother was a mid-wife in the Elk Creek community of Mingo County, West Virginia. A legendary Appalachian "Granny Woman" she is said to have delivered nearly every baby in her "holler" for three generations. Though she held no medical degree, her knowledge was built upon a hodgepodge mixture of practicality, necessity, and to some degree witchcraft.

Though I pride this area on being frozen in time, fortunately, there are many things in the mountains of "downhome" that have changed drastically for the better over the past several decades and childbearing is perhaps the most notable of them.

Today, when a woman discovers she is pregnant, one of the first things she does is schedule an appointment with one of a dozen or more doctors in her community and is soon on a regimental schedule for monthly checkups at the local medical center — but this was a far cry from being so in the mountains only a century ago.

Midwives were not called on until the due date was approaching or labor pains began. Prior to these moments, the women were often left to their own devices or the advice of a relative.

In an era in which herbs served as medication for most everything, pregnant women were encouraged to drink raspberry leaf tea in order to strengthen the uterus.

As the expected date of delivery neared, family members would earnestly pray for the baby to not be born during a full moon, as it was considered highly dangerous to the child and the mother.

The proximity of the midwife to the woman's house would determine when she would arrive — the greater the distance, the earlier she would arrive.

As the days neared, additional relatives would gather at the family's homeplace to celebrate the anticipated arrival of the family's newest member — soon an almost festive atmosphere existed at the home.

In an era long before epidurals, once the woman entered the unspeakably painful state of childbirth, the women of the family would attend to the birthing process, while the men would socialize in another part of the home or out on the porch if the weather permitted.

If the child was not in a proper position, midwives would attempt to manipulate the child by hand. Women were allowed to labor in a sitting position if they felt that was more comfortable for them.

In the event that the labor process was not happening fast enough, midwives had an entire arsenal of tools at their disposal designed to expedite things — these practices included having the pregnant woman ingest turpentine or gunpowder.

Sneezing would also help this process and in order to aid her in sneezing, her caretakers would blow red pepper or gunpowder through a quill into her nose (a practice known as "quilling").

Labor could also be quickened by placing a snakeskin around the thigh. A sharp object placed under the bed was believed to "cut" the labor pains or stop hemorrhaging. An ax could also substitute, however, one that had cut many trees was considered to be the best.

Should the labor end unfortunately, a number of omens and hexes could have been to blame — the mother could have raised her hands above her head, a dove may have mourned outside the window, or a member of the household had swept the steps after sundown.

After a successful birth, the placenta was diligently cared for by taking it into the family's yard and burying it deep enough so that it would not be dug up by humans or animals. If the placenta were dug up, this would bring bad luck, illness, or death to the mother and child. Sometimes the placenta were buried or disposed of in a stream of running water to prevent fever in the mother.

If the mother suffered from an inflammation of her breasts due to the infection of mastitis, treatment would include spreading cow manure on the woman's breasts or cabbage leaves.

Newborns were held upside down by their feet and lifted up and down to prevent 'livergrown' disorder. Some midwives believed that placing the child next to the mother under the quilt would force 'bold hives' out of the baby's body. Others recommended a little catnip or ground ivy tea, a drop or two of turpentine, or a spoonful of whiskey in order to "hive" the baby.

In order to protect the baby's naval area, a piece of cloth would be tied around the newborn's waist for six weeks.

The newborn's hair could not be cut for a specific length of time, which varied from six months to several years, for fear of death.

If a child, whose hair was cut too early, did not die, it was feared that the child would become a thief later in life. If someone stepped over the child, this would stunt the newborn's growth.

Lastly, woe unto the child born on a Tuesday, as these particular children were said to have been unlucky.

Warts, Their Curse, Removal and Omens

Buying Warts

A handful of months ago, a small wart appeared on the side of my right hand. Other than being slightly embarrassing, it really hasn't bothered me too much and for the most part it has remained largely unnoticed.

Unfortunately, yesterday afternoon I spent some time with the honest four-year-old boy next door and he was kind enough to tell me, "the bump on your hand is disgusting."

It pains me to state that hearing the truth out of the mouth of a babe somewhat troubled me — no one wants to walk around town looking "disgusting" and so I dropped by the house of the one person I knew was most capable on offering true, real, and practical advice regarding all things medical — my West Virginia granny!

"Granny, how does a person get rid of a wart?" I asked, expecting for her to give me some type of ointment or provide a recipe to some sassafras-based concoction the old timers from her day used.

"You got a wart?" she inquired.

"Yes," I responded, raising my hand and showing it to her.

Without saying a word, she stood to her feet, reached into her purse and pulled out a shiny quarter and handed it to me.

"I'll buy your wart from you," she answered.

A bit confused, I questioned, "What do you mean?"

"I have an ability to buy warts from people..."

Turns out, she practices a long celebrated mountain superstition in which certain individuals are believed to be able to actually "purchase" a wart from someone and in doing so, make the skin infection disappear.

"Your uncle once had a terrible place on his elbow that wouldn't go away — we had tried everything possible to make it disappear and nothing worked. But then an old man told me that I needed to see if I had the power to buy the wart from him and so I gave it a try and within a week's time of me buying it, that bad place was gone," she recalled, with a certainty so convincing I would have been willing to pay her if she had asked.

After a little bit of research, I discovered that our forefathers were almost obsessed with warts and given the fact that early settlers didn't necessarily practice the greatest hygiene habits, the tiny skin tumors that appear via germs entering cuts and scratches were far more rampant than in modern times.

Unaware of their causes, our ancestors developed various lures pertaining as to why they sprang up (surely, you remember your mother telling you not to touch toads or you'd get warts), and often even more elaborate practices regarding how to rid oneself from the "disgusting" skin bumps.

These practices ranged from washing hands in water that had been used to boil eggs to rubbing a wart with a bean pod and then secretly bury the pod — as the pod rotted and disappeared, so would the wart.

The belief in buying warts, however, can be traced back to Old England, to an era when individuals believed that if someone fell ill, it was the work of an evil spirit troubling them.

In order to confuse the evil spirit troubling their sick children, parents would often "sell" their sons or daughters to a neighbor in hopes that the plaguing spirit would soon become confused and not know where or how to trouble the child.

Over the course of time, this practice evolved from selling one's children to selling one's warts.

***

Notes from the Doctor: Curing Warts & Whooping Cough
The following article was written by Dr. Henry R. Ford, in the Meyer Brothers Druggist, in 1907.

There seems to be more superstitions in this country about warts than on any other one subject... one way to cure them is to take a string and tie a knot in it for every wart which you have. Then pick each wart till it bleeds and put a drop of blood from each wart on a knot. Bury the string and when it rots the wart will get well.

Another superstition in regard to the cure of warts is to take a pebble from under the eaves of house and rub it around a wart three times. Then give it to the person having the warts and let him hide it in the eaves drip of a house and the warts will go away.

While riding through the hills one day, I was hailed while passing a cabin and upon going in, found that the dozen or so children at the place were suffering from the whooping cough.

I made my way in through the gaping, whooping crowd of tow headed youngsters and took a seat by the fireplace.

Sitting on the floor was one of the smaller children trying to cough and eat bread and milk from a bowl with a spoon, while one of the older girls held a very dirty old black cat near.

The child would take a spoonful and then give the cat some from the same spoon.

Upon inquiry I learned that they believed that this was a cure for whooping cough

Old Christmas: The Night Animals Talk

Photo courtesy of Ernst Vikne

January 6, is Christmas Eve night, or at least it would have been had the powers that be, during the Renaissance Period, left our calendars alone, only if they'd done so, January 6 would be December 25.

Confused? I can't ever begin to imagine why!

Allow us to make sense of all this crazy talk:

The development of the Julian Calendar some 2000+ years ago helped standardize the 365-day year and put most of the world's nations onto the same calendar; however, it had one major flaw – it did not take into account the fact that a year is actually 365.2425 days in length. Hence it had no leap years.

Initially, this wasn't that big of a deal, but by the late-1500s, the seasons were really beginning to get messed up and if left unchecked, in a short matter of time, months would be completely out of their respective seasons.

To rescue the calendar and to get things back on track, in 1582 Pope Gregory XIII made the decision to remove 10 days from the calendar.

Though the Pope's edict was initially only accepted by Spain, Portugal, France, Poland, and Italy, in the centuries ahead, one by one, all the kingdoms of Europe followed suit, and in 1752 even Protestant Great Britain adopted the internationally accepted change, moving their calendar ahead eleven days in order to catch up with the rest of the world.

However, the Crown's decision to leap from March 25 to April 5 overnight in 1752 was not well received by the mountain folk across the pond in what is now the Appalachian Mountains of America.

Staunchly anti-Catholic, the fiercely independent Scots-Irish who had, by the mid-1700s, began settling the Appalachians were adamantly opposed to the notion of embracing a new calendar — a new calendar invented by Catholics and adopted by some distant government on the far side of the ocean. The people of the mountains were unwilling to allow the government "to steal eleven days" from their lives.

Christmas had long been observed a handful of weeks after the winter solstice and many of the mountain settlers were unwilling to celebrate the holiday just a few days past autumn.

So what did they do?

They celebrated Christmas, on the old December 25, which due to the Crown adding days into the calendar had become January 7.

Even after the American continent – including Appalachia – embraced the new calendar, the practice of celebrating "Old Christmas" in the mountains continued on for generations.

Nearly all of the modern Christmas traditions we know today were born during the 1800s, and it was during this time that the sons of many of the Appalachian mountianmen surrendered to celebrating on the new date, the new December 25.

Today, there remain a few holdouts who continue to celebrate "Old Christmas" in the Appalachian hills; however, they are a dwindling number. In another generation or two, celebrating "Old Christmas" will probably be just another forgotten part of Appalachian history.

Lost too, are the beliefs that accompany Old Christmas, including my favorite:

On the night before Old Christmas, animals develop supernatural powers, giving them the ability to kneel and even speak.

As an old Kentucky poem about Old Christmas proclaims:
"They's heaps o' folks here still believe,
On Christmas – that's Old Christmas – Eve,
The elders bloom upon the ground,
And critters low and kneel around,
In every stall, though none I know
Has seen them kneel, or heard them low…"

A word of caution, however, to that soul who may be tempted to go outside once the Appalachian sun sets this evening in hopes of listening to a cow, horse or dog speak — it was believed to have been bad luck to ever overhear animals speaking on Old Christmas Eve.

Have a good night Appalachia. And yes, have a very merry [Old] Christmas!

New Year Superstitions

Photo: Mountain family in Anderson County, Tennessee, 1921.

My city-slicker grandmother who did not grow up in the mountains of West Virginia, recalled with a twinkle in her eye, the first time she had New Year's dinner with my grandfather's family in the coalfields of Southern West Virginia.

"I remember sitting down and they brought out a big pot of cooked cabbage and each person had a cabbage roll plopped down onto their plate... About five minutes into dinner, I took a bite and it felt like I had put something metal into my mouth.

"Trying my best to retain the lady-like charm I was raised in the Tidewater to believe I possessed, I quietly excused myself from the table and soon found what appeared to be a dime spit into my napkin..."

Though at first she was baffled as to how a dime had found its way into her dinner, she soon underwent her first of many lessons in Appalachia 101.

In the years ahead, she would come to embrace the mountain tradition of eating cabbage on the first day of the year, though she never completely bought into the idea of hiding a silver coin in one of the rolls for good luck to the unsuspecting individual who found it!

"Why not eat cabbage on the first day of the year," she once quipped, "all the stores in West Virginia have it on sale the day before New Year's."

But where did this seemingly bizarre mountain tradition come from and what does it signify?

Turns out, like so many other aspects of Appalachian tradition and culture, this New Year's practice was born more out of necessity than convenience.

With many mountain families growing the vast majority of the food they consumed all the way up to a generation ago, by mid-winter, cabbage was often the staple vegetable – keeping considerably longer through the cold months than most other veggies and being significantly cheaper made this the ideal New Year's food for a large family.

Over the course of time, this unassuming custom would grow into a tradition in the mountains.

In the years ahead, the Scots-Irish who settled large portions of Appalachia (or kept it from being settled!) married the dinner with an old-world custom of hiding various coins in cooking mashed potatoes with kale or cabbage on special occasions and holidays – the recipient of which would be blessed in the year ahead.

It is important to note that this tradition requires a pure silver coin, not a clad coin as most are today.

First Footer

Another New Year tradition observed throughout the mountains was one known as "First Footer".

This superstition taught that if the first person to set foot in your house in the new year was a tall and dark haired man, you would have good luck awaiting you in the coming year.

The tradition's origins seem to be traced to the Scottish highlands and North England.

Although it is acceptable for the first-foot to be a resident of the house, tradition states that they must not be in the house at the stroke of midnight in order to be the first-foot. Thus, going out of the house after midnight and then coming back into the same house is not considered to be first-footing. It is said to be desirable for the first-foot to be a tall, dark-haired male; a female or fair-haired male are in some places regarded as unlucky.

The South's Black Eyed Peas

Back when I was a kid, as remains the case today, tradition is important and what better time to celebrate timeless rituals than at the beginning of a New Year.

January 1st represents a time of fresh beginnings and new opportunities.

The days get longer with each passing sunrise and there is a new hope that no matter what evils the previous years wrought, the change of the calendar may also bring a change of fortunes.

When it comes to tradition on New Year's, the granddaddy of them all is without a doubt the annual eating of black-eyed peas.

Known in the Deep South as "Hoppin' John", black-eyed peas were typically cooked on New Year's Day with some type of pork product for flavoring.

There are several legends as to the origin of this Southern custom, but the predominate thought dates back to the American Civil War.

It is believed that when Union General William T. Sherman led his army on their infamous "march to the sea", during which time they pillaged the Southland's food supply, that the advancing Yankee soldiers who ransacked a countless number of southern farms were unaware of what black eyed peas even were.

Believing the dried caches to be animal food that was unfit for human consumption, the hungry Union soldiers did not steal these stockpiles as they move farther south.

Southerners considered themselves lucky to be left with enough provisions to help them survive the winter, and black-eyed peas became celebrated throughout the South as a token of great luck, representing prosperity and Divine protection.

It is for this very reason that many southern families still eat black eyed peas on New Year's.

When the Devil Beats His Wife

From the very earliest days of recorded history, humans have had a strong bend toward all things superstitious and when it comes to the many forces of nature – especially weather – this has proven to be even the more true. Perhaps these superstitions were birthed out of a deep-seeded desire to explain the unexplainable or perhaps many of these beliefs began as simple tall tales that caught on somewhere along the way, but regardless, the story of us is rife with incredible and outlandish explanations concerning the day to day events of life.

Of all the meteorological phenomena in the world, the sunshower sits among the top in the number of superstitious beliefs associated with it.

For those of you who may not have grown up somewhere past that county line, a sunshower is the term used to describe the event of rain falling while the sun is shining.

Sunshowers are usually the result of accompanying winds associated with a rain storm sometimes miles away, blowing the airborne raindrops into an area where there are no clouds, therefore causing a sunshower. At other times, a sunshower is created when a single rain cloud passes overhead, and the Sun's angle keeps the sunlight from being obstructed by overhead clouds. Sunshower conditions often lead to the appearance of a rainbow, if the sun is at a low enough angle.

Although widely used throughout the English speaking world, the term "sunshower" is rarely found in dictionaries.

The first bit of "old timer's wisdom" I ever heard about a sunshower was that it was important to take note as to what time it rained that day, as the sunshower meant that it would rain again the following day at the exact same time — though I am aware of no scientific experiments that have ever been performed in order to prove or disprove this, I have often made a mental note of times it's rained with the sun shining and to the best of my knowledge, the following day has always seen rain around that same time; though I'd certainly refrain from betting the farm on this one!

Other and perhaps more colorful superstitions often focus on the Devil, either getting married or having a marital dispute.

In the Southern United States, a sunshower is traditionally believed to be when the devil is beating his wife with a walking stick because he is angry God created a beautiful day.

The rain is said to be that of his wife's tears.

A local belief from Tennessee is that "the devil is kissing his wife", whereas in Cuba and in France, sunshowers are said to be evidence that one of the devil's daughters is getting married somewhere nearby.

—Part Two—
Haunted Places, Ghost Stories and Strange Evidences

The Mothman Prophesies

***

Large portions of the below account have been made possible thanks to the online encyclopedia, Wikipedia's article titled, "Mothman" and "Silver Bridge". The below section is made available through Creative Common / Share-Alike License. Wikipedia® is a registered trademark of the Wikimedia Foundation, Inc., a non-profit organization dedicated to advancing knowledge.

On November 12, 1966, five men who were digging a grave at a cemetery near Clendenin, West Virginia, claimed to see a man-like figure fly low from the trees over their heads. This is often identified as the first known sighting of what became known as the Mothman.

Shortly thereafter, on November 15, 1966, two young couples from Point Pleasant, Roger and Linda Scarberry and Steve and Mary Mallette, told police they saw a large grey creature whose eyes "glowed red" when the car's headlights picked it up. They described it as a "large flying man with ten-foot wings", following their car while they were driving in an area outside of town known as "the TNT area", the site of a former World War II munitions plant.

During the next few days, other people reported similar sightings. Two volunteer firemen who saw it said it was a "large bird with red eyes". Mason County Sheriff George Johnson commented that he believed the sightings were due to an unusually large heron he termed a "shitepoke".

Contractor Newell Partridge told Johnson that when he aimed a flashlight at a creature in a nearby field its eyes glowed "like bicycle reflectors", and blamed buzzing noises from his television set and the disappearance of his German Shepherd dog on the creature.

Wildlife biologist Dr. Robert L. Smith at West Virginia University told reporters that descriptions and sightings all fit the sandhill crane, a large American crane almost as high as a man with a seven-foot wingspan featuring circles of reddish coloring around the eyes, and that the bird may have wandered out of its migration route. This particular crane was unrecognized at first because it was not native to this region.

Collapse of Silver Bridge

The Silver Bridge was an eyebar-chain suspension bridge built in 1928 and named for the color of its aluminum paint. The bridge carried U.S. Route 35 over the Ohio River, connecting Point Pleasant, West Virginia, and Gallipolis, Ohio.

On December 15, 1967, right at the very height of the many Mothman sightings in Point Pleasant, the Silver Bridge collapsed while it was full of

MOUNTAIN SUPERSTITIONS, GHOST STORIES & HAIN TALES

Photo: The statue of Mothman sculpted by Bob Roach. It's located in Point Pleasant, West Virginia., courtesy of Jason W.

rush-hour traffic.

The collapse resulted in the deaths of 46 people. Two of the victims were never found.

Investigation of the wreckage pointed to the cause of the collapse being the failure of a single eyebar in a suspension chain, due to a small defect 0.1

inches (2.5 mm) deep. Analysis showed that the bridge was carrying much heavier loads than it had originally been designed for and had been poorly maintained.

The incident gave rise to the legend and connected the Mothman sightings to the bridge collapse.

In 2016, WCHS-TV published a photo purported to be of Mothman taken by an anonymous man while driving on Route 2. Science writer Sharon A. Hill proposed that the photo showed "a bird, perhaps an owl, carrying a frog or snake away" and wrote that "there is zero reason to suspect it is the Mothman as described in legend. There are too many far more reasonable explanations."

Legacy of Mothman

Folklorist Jan Harold Brunvand notes that Mothman has been widely covered in the popular press, some claiming sightings connected with UFOs, and others claiming that a military storage site was Mothman's "home". Brunvand notes that recountings of the 1966-67 Mothman reports usually state that at least 100 people saw Mothman with many more "afraid to report their sightings" but observed that written sources for such stories consisted of children's books or sensationalized or undocumented accounts that fail to quote identifiable persons.

Brunvand found elements in common among many Mothman reports and much older folk tales, suggesting that something real may have triggered the scares and became woven with existing folklore. He also records anecdotal tales of Mothman supposedly attacking the roofs of parked cars inhabited by teenagers.

Conversely, Joe Nickell says that a number of hoaxes followed the publicity generated by the original reports, such as a group of construction workers who tied flashlights to helium balloons. Nickell attributes the Mothman reports to pranks, misidentified planes, and sightings of a barred owl, an albino owl, suggesting that the Mothman's "glowing eyes" were actually red-eye effect caused from the reflection of light from flashlights or other bright light sources. The area lies outside the snowy owl's usual range.

Some pseudoscience adherents (such as ufologists, paranormal authors, and cryptozoologists) claim that Mothman was an alien, a supernatural manifestation, or a previously unknown species of animal. In his 1975 book *The Mothman Prophecies*, author John Keel claimed that the Point Pleasant residents experienced precognitions including premonitions of the collapse of the Silver Bridge, unidentified flying object sightings, visits from inhuman or threatening men in black, and other phenomena.

Point Pleasant held its first Annual Mothman Festival in 2002 and a 12-foot-tall metallic statue of the creature, created by artist and sculptor Bob Roach, was unveiled in 2003. The Mothman Museum and Research Center opened in 2005 and is run by Jeff Wamsley. The Festival is a weekend-long event held on the 3rd weekend of every September. There is a variety of events that go on during the festival such as guest speakers, vendor exhibits, a mothman pancake eating contest, and hayride tours focusing on the notable areas of Point Pleasant.

The Moon-Eyed People

The Cherokee have a longstanding oral history that includes tales of what they refer to as "The Moon-Eyed People."

According to their accounts, the moon-eyed people are an extinct race of people who were said to have lived in Appalachia until the Cherokee expelled them. They were received their name because for whatever reason, saw better at nighttime than during the day.

Accounts of this mysterious group of people date back to 1797 when Benjamin Smith Barton, who explained their existence to readers back in Europe.

Some accounts of the moon-eyed people declare that they had white skin and following their defeat by the Cherokee went west.

***

In 1900, James Moone published a book entitled, "Myths of the Cherokee", which records various oral histories handed down by the Cherokees

The earliest reference appears to be that of Barton in 1797, on the statement of a gentleman whom he quotes as a valuable authority upon the southern tribes.

"The Cherokee tell us, that when they first arrived in the country which they inhabit, they found it possessed by certain 'moon-eyed people,' who could not see in the day-time. These wretches they expelled."

He seems to consider them an albino race. Haywood, twenty-six years later, says that the invading Cherokee found "white people" near the head of the Little Tennessee, with forts extending thence down the Tennessee as far as Chickamauga creek. He gives the location of three of these forts. The Cherokee made war against them and drove them to the mouth of Big Chickamauga Creek, where they entered into a treaty and agreed to remove if permitted to depart in peace. Permission being granted, they abandoned the country.

Elsewhere he speaks of this extirpated white race as having extended into Kentucky and probably also into western Tennessee, according to concurrent traditions of different tribes. He describes their houses... as having been small circular structures of upright logs, covered with earth which had been dug out from the inside.

Harry Smith [Half Cherokee, Half White] was born about 1815, father of the late chief of the East Cherokee, informed the author that when a boy he had been told by an old woman a tradition of a race of very small people, perfectly white, who once came and lived for some time on the site of the ancient mound on the northern side of Hiwassee, at the mouth of

Peachtree Creek, a few miles above the present Murphy, North Carolina. They afterward removed to the West. Colonel Thomas, the white chief of the East Cherokee, born about the beginning of the century, had also heard a tradition of another race of people who lived on Hiwassee, opposite the present Murphy, and warned the Cherokee that they must not attempt to cross over to the south side of the river or the great leech in the water would swallow them. They finally went west, "long before the whites came." The two stories are plainly the same, although told independently and many miles apart.

***

North Carolina Ghosts, a site that has been sharing stories and folklore for over ten years published an article about the Moon-Eyed People, which included the following

Moon-Eyed People are never described as being supernatural, but are remembered as another group of humans who were physically very different than the Native Americans.

Because the description of the Moon-Eyed People is that they are pale-skinned and bearded, this has led to some amount of speculation, quite a bit of it wild, that the legend of the Moon-Eyed People represents a Cherokee folk memory of contact with a group of European settlers who made it to the new world before Columbus. Particularly, the Cherokee legend of the Moon-Eyed People has been matched up with the Welsh legend of Prince Madoc.

According to the Welsh story, Madoc ab Owain Gwynedd was a Welsh prince who, disenchanted with the civil war wracking his homeland, set sail with his brother Rhirid and a few followers in 1170 across the Atlantic Ocean and landed somewhere around Mobile Bay, Alabama. After some exploring up and down the rivers of southern America, Madoc decided he liked the place well enough and decided to move in. Leaving Rhirid and some of his fellow Welshmen behind, Madoc returned to his native country and recruited enough followers to fill ten ships. He and his colonists set sail back to America and was never heard from in Wales again. Some have speculated that the Moon-Eyed People are the descendants of Madoc's colonists, and that it was these Welshman who fought a war with the Cherokee, and these Welshmen who built the stone forts that dot the ridges of the mountains.

Did the Irish Explore America in 500 A.D.?

The previous account concerning the moon-eyed-people offers an excellent bridge into this next topic:

"In 1492, Columbus sailed the ocean blue... and before that time, no European had ever so much as even imagined there being a world beyond the ocean, let alone stepped foot on the continent of North America."

Right?

That's what we were all taught as young and dreamy-eyed school children each October, but what if the long recited narrative is wrong — way wrong?

Enter the field of forbidden history: Part sci-fi, part archeology, part conspiracy theory and 100% fascinating.

Granted, the evidence is shaky and a far cry from being enough to send someone to the gallows over, but as time progresses there is an increasing number of individuals who are seeing evidences in a totally new light and are beginning to question everything you've ever been taught about the history of America.

The modern theory of ancient Irish missionaries appearing in the New World roughly a millennium ago has its origins with an unusual discovery in the coalfields of Southern West Virginia during the early-1980s.

As the story goes, local residents in the tiny community of Dingess, West Virginia, discovered ancient markings and engravings on large boulders near a strip mines.

The slabs of rock, which were found on property owned by the Marrowbone Development Corporation, immediately became the source of study for scholars from around the world, as the markings were said to resemble ancient Irish letters known as Celtic Ogham.

In October of 1988, representatives from the Irish Embassy, including the nation's secretary of cultural affairs met with archaeologist Robert Pyle to examine the ancient rock carvings, referred to as petroglyphs.

Speaking to members of the media, Pyle was quoted as having said, "They're really unique. They have Christian religious symbols that are identifiable, many of them identifiable were recorded very early... The markings appear to be from around as early as the eighth century to the 12th century A.D."

The veteran archaeologist said that he believed the markings were made by early Irish missionaries who followed major trails through the mountains, stating, "It's really a tremendous discovery."

Pyle is not alone in his belief that the Irish were roaming the hills along the Tug Valley centuries prior to Columbus' voyage.

Dr. Barry Fell, a biologist who has studied numerous archaeological sites and ancient languages, contended that ancient West Virginia Petroglyphs were indeed written in the ancient Irish language known as Ogham.

Translating rock markings found in neighboring Wyoming County, West Virginia, Dr. Fell concluded that the ancient message carved into the rocks read: "At the time of sunrise, a ray grazes the notch on the left side on Christmas Day, the first season of the year, the season of the blessed advent of the savior Lord Christ. Behold he is born of Mary, a woman."

But not everyone is convinced — in 1989 lawyers Monroe Oppenheimer and Willard Wirtz wrote an article based on opinions of other archaeologists and linguistic experts, disputing the theory that the inscription is written in Ogham script. They further accused Fell of deliberate fraud, a charge Fell denied.

Regardless of what the West Virginia Petroglyphs turn out to be, there are still numerous unanswered puzzle pieces that seem to beg the question, "Could there actually be something to all to all of this?"

Most notable, is tale of a Celtic missionary who spent his life attempting to convert pagan Ireland to Christianity.

Eventually, this Irish saint embarked on a legendary voyage that some believe took him to North America.

Born in County Kerry in 484 A.D., St. Brendan the Navigator is said to have traveled tirelessly to evangelize and establish monasteries following his ordination to the priesthood at age 28.

"The sixth-century monk frequently sailed the high seas to spread the gospel throughout Ireland as well as to Scotland, Wales and Brittany in the north of France... According to a 1,500-year-old Irish tale, however, St. Brendan embarked on one particularly epic journey in the winter of his 93-year-old life. According to the story, St. Barinthus told St. Brendan that he had just returned from a visit to Paradise, a land that lurked far beyond the horizon. For 40 days St. Brendan fasted and prayed atop a mountain on the rugged Dingle Peninsula, a spindly finger of land on the west of Ireland that points directly at North America.." writes Christopher Klein.

While most considered the narrative of St. Brendan to be nothing more than a religious allegory, there has been considerable discussion as to whether the legends are based at least partly on fact.

Tales through the Middle Ages, long before Columbus's voyage, detail the early missionary's travels and even describe his sailing vessel: a currach-like boat of wattle, covered with hides tanned in oak bark and softened with butter. The boat had a mast and a sail, which protected he and a small group of monks as they traveled beyond the ocean's western horizon.

There have been many interpretations of the possible geographical location of Saint Brendan's Island, if the account is even true, but numerous pre-Columbian sea charts included an island somewhere in the far-western Atlantic known simply as St. Brendan's Island.

British historian, explorer and writer Tim Severin demonstrated that it is possible for a leather-clad boat, such as the one described in the tale of St. Brendan, to reach North America.

The story was known widely in Europe throughout the Middle Ages and some historians argue that Christopher Columbus learned from the account that the currents and winds would favor westbound travel by a southerly route from the Canary Islands, and eastbound on the return trip by a more northerly route, and hence followed this itinerary on all of his voyages.

Other tales state that when the Spanish began exploring the New World in what is now North and South Carolina, they came in contact with a mysterious tribe of natives known as the Duhares.

According to an article penned by Kerry O'Shea last year, "Physically, the people of Duhare appeared to be European according to the Spanish colonists in the area. The people of Duhare had red to brown hair, tan skin and gray eyes, and were noticeably taller than the Spanish. According to Spanish accounts, the people of Duhare were Caucasian, though their houses and pottery were similar to those of American Indians…"

O'Shea writes, that roughly a decade ago a team of researchers attempted to record every single Native American word that was translated by the Spanish. "While many of those words were easily translated by modern Creek, Alabama, Koasati or Choctaw dictionaries, the words associated with the province of Duhare defied translation until 2011… Researchers began to investigate the similarity of Irish rock carvings to those in the state of South Carolina. One member of the [team] came across an ancient Irish lullaby entitled 'Bainne nam fiadh' – 'On milk of deer I was reared. On milk of deer I was nurtured. On milk of deer beneath the ridge of storms on crest of hill and mountain.' The lullaby has particular significance as the deer were a prominent resource for Duhare people. According to Spanish sources, the Duhare maintained large herds of domesticated deer and made cheese from deer milk. The excess male deer population was fattened with corn for butchering."

Granted, all of these legends, tall tales and mysteries aren't quite enough to call for the burning of history textbooks, but they certainly cause one to pause and began wondering, "Could it be that history as we know it may not be accurate?"

Southwest Virginia: UFOs & Devil Monkeys

Wytheville, Virginia's UFO Scare

The 1980s and 90s presented some incredibly tall tales in many parts of Appalachia. These wild and hairy stories ranged from the downright bizarre and laughable to more serious and bone chilling claims.

These decades were also known for the introduction of several new mind-altering substances and illicit drugs; it remains to be determined as to what extent these two realities are related!

At the epicenter of Appalachia's dark and unsolved mysteries was Virginia's Ninth Congressional District — a mountainous region wedged between West Virginia, North Carolina, Tennessee and Kentucky. Though the rest of the world may think of Virginia Beach and Arlington when they hear "Virginia" mentioned, for those of us 'round here, our mind is transported to a steep mountainside in late-November or a humid hayfield on the hottest July afternoon when we hear mention of our beloved state. This area is known locally as Southwest Virginia, but I will never call it by any other name than home.

Ordinarily comprised of quiet and hardworking farming communities, this region buzzed to life and was propelled to the national stage when I was a young boy.

I was just a child in the 1980s, living past the town limit sign of Wytheville, Virginia, on a 300-acre Black Angus farm; however, despite my young age at the time, I still remember very vividly piling into the back of our family's black Dodge Ram pickup truck and bouncing through the cow pastures to the quietness afforded on "the back side" of our family farm.

There on the "Back Side", we were miles from the nearest lights and free to gaze into the sky in hopes of seeing one of the mysterious UFOs so many of our friends and neighbors swore they had seen.

That one year, though I do not remember exactly which one it was, our entire small town went UFO crazy, thanks to an incident that could be traced back to a handful of local sheriff's deputies, who reported seeing mysterious lights traveling through the nighttime sky.

Military veterans, the officers who made those initial sightings stated emphatically that what they saw was nothing close to being a light from an airplane, even though that's what many locals initially accused them of seeing.

This report set the stage for a countless number of additional sightings that soon had our town captivated by the idea that we were possibly being visited by aliens from beyond our solar system.

In the days ahead, a popular radio news broadcaster in our town reported the sightings and soon a flood of calls inundated the radio station from townspeople saying they, too, had seen the same mysterious lights.

In the weeks that followed, Wytheville would be visited by numerous journalists, photographers and curiosity seekers, each in search of their own UFO story – many of which were successful in going home with a story that could neither be corroborated or denied.

As a boy, I spent many afternoons that year sitting beside my father in the local gun store listening to he and so many other men of the town swap stories of what they had seen and debate who among them was telling the truth and who was "more full of it than a Christmas turkey!"

By the saga's conclusion, local residents would be recanting their stories on *Unsolved Mysteries*, a show whose intro music and chilling voice of the narrator still has me wanting to run to my bedroom in fear, just as it did some thirty years ago!

In the episode that finally aired, friends and neighbors would claim to have damning photos of mysterious objects which they claimed were stolen by officials believed to have been representing the United States government. As convenient and unbelievable as their stories may be, there are many evidences that could point to the fact that they may have some validity to their words.

During this time period, the clouded memory of my childhood still recalls a story my father told to our family as he stepped into our vehicle after paying for gas at the fill-up station.

With tears in his eyes from having laughed so hard, he said, still gasping for breath from laughter, "That ole lady in thur working the counter was telling all of us that she seen'd a UFO las' night."

Going on, he said, "She looked right up at us and said – as serious as a heart-attack – 'I know'd it was a UFO because right on the side of h'it, h'it said U-F-O!'"

Eventually the town that was featured on Robert Stack's *Unsolved Mysteries* would move on with life. The coming 1990s would bring Garth Brooks, the Internet and NAFTA – whatever exactly that was – and barely a decade later, September 11th would transform all of our thinking until we reached a point that

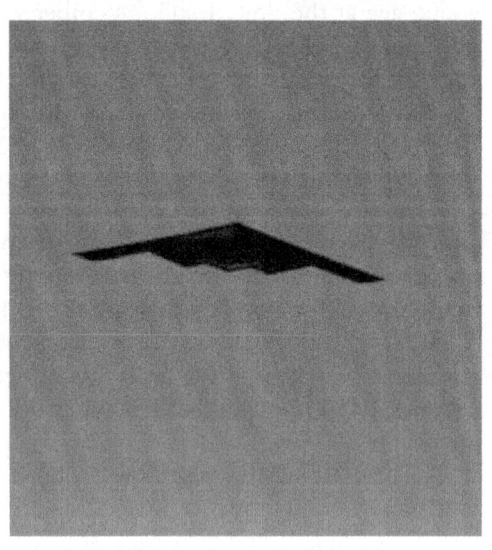

PHOTO: US Air Force B-2 Stealth Bomber, courtesy of Prayitno

for many of us the UFO craze was a distant and largely forgotten memory and now many newcomers to town or younger people don't even know about the pandemic that once swept our little community.

These days, in Wytheville, talk about that season of UFO mania is a largely taboo subject in most circles; only whispered about softly, inside a busy restaurant so as not to be overheard by the wrong person – you never know who's related to who in a town like ours!

But before we rip on the community too much for what they claim to have seen, we must remember that several individuals in the late-1980s reported seeing mysterious unidentified flying objects that were often described as being triangular in shape, very quiet and very "stealthy".

Though the United States Air Force has never released any official statements concerning the Wytheville UFO craze, one can't help but recognize that the planes unveiled at the onset of the Persian Gulf War bore a very close similarity to what many local farmers described seeing only a handful of years earlier.

Virginia's Black Devil Monkey

One of the more entertaining stories to spring forth from this region was one woman's claim to have spotted a mysterious black "devil monkey" in Roanoke, Virginia, in 1994.

According to multiple sources, an Ohio woman was driving through Roanoke around 2:30 a.m. when a construction detour sent her down a dark two-lane country road.

As she drove the wilderness terrain of Southwest Virginia, a creature that looked like a hybrid wolf-monkey reportedly leapt in front of her car.

One Internet source described the creature as being "all black with very short sleek fur, pointy ears and had a long thin tail…"

The woman described the creature as being catlike, and yet not like any cat to which she was familiar.

Having seen the creature standing on its back legs, the woman guessed its height to be about 6-ft. tall and she adamantly argued that its "torso looked very much like that of a very thin man and its head resembled a man almost with a pointy beard. However, the creature's hind legs were like a wild cat or dog. It was very muscular and thin."

The woman later shared her story with US Game & Wildlife officials who insisted it must have been a feral dog or wolf, but the woman was emphatic that the creature she saw was neither of the two.

A few weeks following the woman's ordeal, livestock in the area around the location where the alleged sighting was began disappearing.

Granted, this seems like a bizarre story that could easily be attributed to midnight AM talk radio and a case of some bad gas station coffee; however, it is interesting to note that about thirty-five years earlier, just down US

Route 11 in Smyth County, Virginia, various individuals claimed to have spotted nearly the exact same creature.

In 1959, a couple driving down a back road in Saltville, Virginia, reportedly had their car attacked by a large, powerful creature they claimed chased their vehicle and left deep scratches along the door.

The online blog, FRONTIERS OF ZOOLOGY, describes the couple's ordeal in detail below:

"According to their account, an ape-like beast attacked their car, leaving three scratch marks on the vehicle... [the couple's daughter] described the terrifying attacker: 'It had light, taffy colored hair, with a white blaze down its neck and underbelly... it stood on two, large well-muscled back legs and had shorter front legs or arms.'"

A handful of years later, an almost exact same claim was made in the same community when two nurses from the Saltville area were driving home from work one morning and were reportedly attacked by an unknown creature whom they stated ripped the convertible top from their car. Luckily the nurses — though surely frightened out of their wits — were unharmed.

The mysterious monkey-wolf hybrid beast would come to be known as "the devil monkey" and in the decades that followed, numerous alleged sightings of these animals were reported.

In recent years, devil monkey sightings have waned, but from time to time, an occasional sighting of these mysterious creatures is quietly whispered about in corner barbershops or over an Appalachian campfire.

The Martha Washington Inn & Spa

PHOTO: The Martha Washington Inn & Spa, Appalachian Magazine

Established in the 1700s as a final stop along the Wilderness Road, the settlement of Abingdon, Virginia, has been entertaining travelers longer than the United States of America has been a sovereign country. The historic brick buildings and taverns that line US Route 11, the town's Main Street, bear record of the area's rich past -- a history that local leaders have taken great pains to protect and preserve through the years.

The reason for their stays has changed drastically over the centuries, but even some 250 years later, Abingdon is still thriving thanks to the travel industry.

Today, visitors to this charming and quaint Southwest Virginia community aren't looking to make final purchases before crossing through the Cumberland Gap, but instead come seeking something just as valuable: peace of mind and an escape from the pressures and realities of life. Fortunately for them, Virginia's Blue Ridge Highlands offer endless acres of this very commodity.

In this region of the state, visitors can choose from any number of lodging accommodations, ranging from yurts to cabins to hotels and guests to this mountainous enclave can even lose themselves in a live performance at Barter Theatre, the State Theatre of Virginia; not to mention the incredible feeling that accompanies dining inside a building that predates the American Civil War by several decades.

All of these things are wonderful, but when it comes to selecting the perfect getaway, hands down, the flagship luxury hotel in Southwest Virginia is The Martha Washington Inn & Spa.

Visitors to this 63-room inn enjoy the unique opportunity to step back in time to an era of excessive luxury, without sacrificing any of the modern day conveniences we have come to expect in the twenty-first century.

My wife and I recently stayed at The Martha Washington and though we have spent many nights at a countless number of resorts, B&Bs and hotels, thanks to *Appalachian Magazine*, very few are comparable to this Appalachian gem.

Our stay began with us taking Interstate 81's Exit 17 and within a few hundred yards from the highway, we were no longer lost in the web of massive billboards and chain restaurants which sadly serve as the landscape of the average Interstate town. Abingdon is different. The downtown area is protected as a historic district, which ensures no ugly billboards or chain stores. The brick sidewalks, stone curbs and red bricked buildings have a way of transporting one's mind back to a forgotten and largely unknown time period -- an era just about all of us seem to hunger for from time to time.

As one of our readers so wonderfully described it, "Abingdon is not one of those places where you go to learn history, but rather, where you go to feel history."

Simply driving onto the property of what was originally built in 1832 to serve as a home for Congressman Francis Preston and his family, I could feel my senses being altered -- I was traveling through time.

As the main doors opened into the lobby of the historic inn, I could again feel my mind being rushed back to another era: This time to the antebellum period when the building served as Martha Washington College, an higher learning institution devoted entirely to women which operated for seventy years until the hardships of the Great Depression forced the Appalachian women's college to shutter its doors.

During the Civil War, the college served as the training ground for a Confederate unit known as the Washington Mounted Rifles and after a number of fights and skirmishes between Yankee and Rebel forces, the girls of the school treated the battle wounded, it was also during this time period that the building attained the nickname, "The Martha."

As is the case with just about all old and historic buildings, the Internet is rife with tales of jaded lovers, murdered Confederate soldiers and past students who now frequent The Martha Washington as ghosts. To be quite honest, we never felt anything spooky or of another dimension while we were there; however, the unmistaken energy that accompanies being in a place where so much history has occurred is undeniable -- it isn't every day that one gets to sleep in a place which was the family home of a 1700s Congressman, antebellum women's college, Civil War hospital, and famous hotel whose guests include Eleanor Roosevelt, President Harry Truman, Lady Bird Johnson, President Jimmy Carter, and Elizabeth Taylor.

Though we felt nothing and saw nothing, below are the many tales of ghosts and sprits circulating concerning The Martha Washington Inn & Spa.

***

Large portions of the below accounts have been made possible thanks to the online encyclopedia, Wikipedia's article titled, "Martha Washington Inn". The below section is made available through Creative Common / Share-Alike License. Wikipedia® is a registered trademark of the Wikimedia Foundation, Inc., a non-profit organization dedicated to advancing knowledge.

The Yankee Sweetheart

This story is about a tragic love affair between a student at Martha Washington College and her Yankee sweetheart. Although still a girl's college, Martha Washington College served as a hospital during the Civil War. Several of the girls did not return home during the war, but bravely volunteered to stay at the school as nurses.

Captain John Stoves, a Yankee officer, was severely wounded and captured in town. Soldiers carried Capt. Stoves through the cave system under Abingdon and up a secret stairway to the third floor of the building. Capt. Stoves lay gravely wounded in what is now Room 403.

For weeks, a young student named Beth nursed and cared for him.

She found herself falling in love with the brave captain, and he returned her sentiments.

Often, Beth would lovingly play the violin to ease his pain and suffering. But, their love was not to last for long. As he lay dying, he called, "Play something, Beth, I'm going."

Unfortunately, Beth was too late to escort him out with a song, because he died suddenly.

Beth tearfully played a sweet southern melody as a tribute to him.

When a Confederate officer entered and explained that he was taking Captain Stoves as a prisoner, Beth faced him triumphantly and said, "He has been pardoned by an officer higher than General Lee. Captain Stoves is dead."

Beth died a few weeks later from typhoid fever.

Many of the female students who later attended the college, as well as inn employees and guests, have heard Beth's sweet violin music in the night.

Others report that Beth visits Room 403 to comfort her Yankee soldier.

PHOTO: The Martha Washington Inn & Spa, Appalachian Magazine

Reappearing Bloodstain

A young Confederate soldier in Abingdon was assigned to carry important papers about the location of the Union army to General Robert E. Lee. He was hopelessly in love with a young woman at the college.

Knowing the risks he was facing, the brave soldier felt he must say farewell to his lady love before leaving. The soldier traveled through the cave system underlying Abingdon and used a secret stairway to enter the college.

As the soldier was saying goodbye to his love, two Union officers came up the stairs and found them. With no way to escape, the young Confederate soldier was shot in front of his sweetheart, and, when he fell, his blood stained the floor.

The strange thing is that through the years, the bloodstain continues to appear. Carpets over the area often develop mysterious holes over the stains. Even after the floors have been refinished, the stain continues to reappear, a sad reminder of the tragedy of the Civil War.

Phantom Horse

A young Confederate soldier in Abingdon was assigned to carry important papers about the location of the Union army to General Robert E. Lee. He was hopelessly in love with a young woman at the college. Knowing the risks he was facing, the brave soldier felt he must say farewell to his lady love before leaving. The soldier traveled through the cave system underlying Abingdon and used a secret stairway to enter the college. As the soldier was saying goodbye to his love, two Union officers came up the stairs and found them. With no way to escape, the young Confederate soldier was shot in front of his sweetheart, and, when he fell, his blood stained the floor. The strange thing is that through the years, the bloodstain continues to appear. Carpets over the area often develop mysterious holes over the stains. Even after the floors have been refinished, the stain continues to reappear, a sad reminder of the tragedy of the Civil War.

The Trail Of Mud

Numerous accounts of a soldier hobbling with help from a crutch and leaving a trail of mud in his wake have been reported from a hallway of the Inn. Long past medical help, there is only speculation why he is here at the old hospital, a ball leaving only a hideous mangle of bone and sparse flesh had split his head.

The Angry Spirit In The Tunnel

An underground tunnel once connected the Martha Washington Inn with the Barter Theatre. The entrance on the inn's side has been closed off for several years, but the section below the theater is still used to run electrical cables. Actors who used the tunnel to walk between the inn and the theater in the 1930s and 1940s reported encountering a malevolent spirit. The specter was never seen but sensed as a strong evil presence. The spirit is believed to be either a man who was killed when the tunnel collapsed in 1890 or a Confederate soldier who used the tunnel to smuggle ammunition out of the inn's basement during the Civil War.

The Greenbrier Ghost

*This article is courtesy of
Dave Tabler/AppalachianHistory.net*

On January 23, 1897, Elva Zona Heaster Shue of Lewisburg, West Virginia, a bride of three months, was found dead at the bottom of the stairs leading to the second floor of the log house where she lived with her new husband. Her body was discovered by a neighbor, a boy of about 11 years, who did chores for her. Her case remains to this day a one of a kind event in the American judicial system ... the only case in which the word of a ghost helped to solve a crime and convict a murderer!

A state highway marker several miles west of town sums up Shue's amazing story: "Interred in a nearby cemetery is Zona Heaster Shue. Her death in 1897 was presumed natural until her spirit appeared to her mother to describe how she was killed by her husband Edward. Autopsy on the exhumed body verified the apparition's account. Edward, found guilty of murder, was sentenced to state prison."

Upon finding the dead woman, Andy Jones, the neighbor boy, ran back to his home where he informed his mother, and then continued on to the blacksmith shop where Edward S. Shue was working. When told of the situation Shue appeared in great anguish, ran to his home, gathered his dead wife into his arms, and directed local doctor and coroner, Dr. George W. Knapp, be called. All during this time Shue held Zona's head in his arms. After a brief examination, Dr. Knapp concluded that Zona "died of an everlasting faint," i.e. a heart attack.

Photo: Elva Zona Heaster Shue

The body was prepared for burial with Shue assisting in the preparation of her body for burial, and placing her in the casket, always handling her head. He placed a folded sheet on one side of her head and an article of clothing on the other side of her head, which he said would make her rest easier. In addition, he tied a large scarf around her neck and explained tearfully that it "had been Zona's favorite."

Zona was taken to the home of her mother, Mrs. Mary Jane Heaster, on nearby Big Sewell Mountain. When the casket was opened Shue always remained at the head of the casket. The next day her body was buried in the little cemetery on the hill top. Nothing more was thought of the death other than that usual for a sudden death of anyone.

Within a month of the burial, however, the dead girl's mother was telling neighbors that Zona's spirit had appeared four nights in a row to accuse the blacksmith of her violent death – to "tell on him" – to set the record straight about her dying. Shue had been abusive and cruel, she said, and had attacked her in a fit of rage, savagely breaking her neck. Word spread quickly that these visions had convinced Mary Jane that the husband – who called himself Edward, but was really named Erasmus Stribbling Trout Shue, and was known as 'Trout' – had killed her daughter.

Photo: House where the murder took place.

Mary Heaster and her brother-in-law Johnson Heaster went to Lewisburg prosecutor John A. Preston, who first disbelieved the story, but after several hours of questioning Mrs. Heaster became convinced that there was a basis for an investigation.

Dr. Knapp was consulted and he agreed that he might have been mistaken in his diagnosis. An investigation into Shue's background revealed that he had served a term in the penitentiary and had been married twice previously, and both wives had died under strange circumstances. One wife was supposed to have died from a broken neck when she fell from a haystack. The other wife died while helping Shue to repair a chimney. He was on top of the chimney and his wife was placing the rocks in a basket with a rope attached to it and as the basket was drawn up the basket turned and dropped the rock on the head of his wife.

An exhumation was ordered and an inquest jury was assembled. *The Greenbrier Independent* reported that Trout Shue "vigorously complained" about the exhumation but it was made clear to him that he would be forced to attend the inquest if he did not go willingly. In rebuttal he replied that he knew that he would be arrested, "but they will not be able to prove I did it." This careless statement indicated that he at least had knowledge that his wife had been murdered.

The autopsy findings were quite damning to Shue. An *Independent* report on March 9 said that "the discovery was made that the neck was broken and the windpipe mashed. On the throat were the marks of fingers indicating that she had been choken [sic]..... the neck was dislocated between the first and second vertebrae. The ligaments were torn and ruptured. The windpipe had been crushed at a point in front of the neck."

The findings were made public at once, upsetting many in the community. Shue was arrested, charged with murder, and taken to the jail at Lewisburg where he was held until his indictment by a Grand Jury and the trial in June.

On June 22, 1897 the jury returned a verdict of guilty after only one hour and ten minutes of deliberation. The accounts in the *Independent* make clear that Shue was convicted of the murder of his third wife on circumstantial evidence, and not because of a "ghost's testimony." He was sentenced to life in the state prison. Following a foiled lynching attempt a few days later, he was taken by train to the state prison in Moundsville, where he died on the first of March, 1900.

North Carolina's Mystery Lights

Like nearly all of Appalachia, the mountains of North Carolina are no stranger to ghost tales, superstitions and good ol'e fashioned haints. However, few places in the Tar Heel State, or the world for that matter, present as many questions or pose as great a mystery to scientists as the centuries of incredible tales about one North Carolina mountain that stands roughly 2,200-ft above sea level.

As with so many Appalachian mysteries, separating fact from folklore can be a daunting task, but for nearly two centuries a countless number of individuals and publications have been swearing that Brown Mountain in the state's western ridges has been scene to multiple showings of mysterious lights – often in the form of what appears to be bouncing balls.

In 1921, Yale University researchers published a report about the phenomenon, stating, "The so called 'Brown Mountain lights' appear at any time between dark and daylight. They are intermittent, spasmodic brilliances, appearing at no fixed point on the ridge and seeming to have no connection with the ground, but rather to float above the trees on the crest. They are not illuminations, but very definite points of radiance, much like the light of a lantern though much larger and more brilliant. They are generally of a clear white color though sometimes doubtless due to atmospheric conditions they appear yellowish and occasionally with a reddish tinge. They are visible from prominent points as far away as 15 miles on clear evenings, visible from all points of the compass, though strangely enough the lookout in his tower does not see them.

"The first explanation gave the lights to be those of the headlights on the locomotives of the Southern Railway which, when they were turned just a certain way flashed toward the observer on his high vantage point. This was good, except that after the 1916 flood the Southern didn't operate a locomotive in that section for two weeks, but the lights were seen just the same."

Other theories presented by Yale University scientists ranged from a rare weather phenomenon known as "St. Elmo's Fire", where a bright blue or violet glow, appearing like fire in some circumstances, from tall, sharply pointed objects. St. Elmo's fire can also appear on leaves and grass, and even at the tips of cattle horns.

Not long after the Yale University article appeared, *National Geographic* reported on the lights, stating that though "the first journalistic account of the phenomenon appeared in 1913, the claim is made locally that these lights have puzzled observers since before the Civil War."

While scientists have sought a logical and scientific explanation, many locals attribute the light display to something more spiritual.

It is has been said that the area played host to a massive battle between the Cherokee and Catawba nations some 300 years prior to the arrival of the first white men to the continent.

Some locals claim that the lights are those of the ghosts of Cherokee widows, holding torches, searching for their husbands.

Over the past decade, sightings of the lights have waned significantly, leading researchers who believe in a scientific or supernatural explanation in agreement that whatever power was creating the lights for a span of centuries appears to be waning.

The most recent scientific explanation is that the lights may be the result of an unexplained atmospheric electrical phenomenon known as ball lightning, in which a spherical object as large as several meters in diameter appears to hover, often lasting considerably longer than the split-second flash of a lightning bolt.

Though the actual cause or even the existence of Brown Mountain, North Carolina's mysterious light show remains a hotly contested debate, one thing is clear — the folks who claim to have seen the lights are not backing down from their stories.

Ball Lightning & St. Elmo's Fire

*In 1922, American Magazine, Volume 94,
published the following report about ball lightning & St. Elmo's Fire:*

Ball lightning is so shrouded with fancy that little is known of it. Some people who say they have seen it declare that they have watched such a ball float slowly into a house through an open door or window and then explode.

Other amazing stories of the vagaries of ball lightning are told. A man familiar with electricity is quoted as relating that he was once compelled to seek shelter from a thunderstorm in a farmhouse. While the storm was raging, he noticed a ball of fire drifting along the ground. It floated gently into a pigpen and bounced off one of the walls.

Finally, a small pig interested in the strange visitant went up and smelled of it. Thereupon it exploded, scattering pig and pen over the landscape.

Most of the stories of ball lightning are probably due to over active imaginations, a natural enough consequence of the excitement of a thunderstorm. Under these conditions, it is rather difficult to observe exactly and carefully.

There are however, a few observations which seem to be beyond challenge. Yet we know so little that no complete explanation of ball lightning can be suggested.

An electrical demonstration that we cannot properly classify as lightning is the silent discharge known as St Elmo's fire. It is the luminous brush of electricity that often plays on the tips of high pointed objects such as the spires of churches and the mases of vessels at sea.

The name comes from St Elmo, the patron saint invoked by mariners in the Mediterranean.

Thunderstorms usually follow two or three days of very warm weather. On land they most frequently develop between two and four o'clock in the afternoon, when the surface of the earth is hottest and the upward rush of warm moist air tends to reach its greatest height and velocity.

On the ocean for reasons a little too scientifically complicated to explain in passing, these storms are likeliest to break between midnight and four o'clock in the morning.

The Rattlesnake's Vengeance

In 1900, James Moone published a book entitled, "Myths of the Cherokee", which records various oral histories handed down by the Cherokees

One day in the old times when we could still talk with other creatures, while some children were playing about the house, their mother inside heard them scream. Running out she found that a rattlesnake had crawled from the grass, and taking up a stick she killed it. The father was out hunting in the mountains, and that evening when coming home after dark through the gap he heard a strange wailing sound. Looking about he found that he had come into the midst of a whole company of rattlesnakes, which all had their mouths open and seemed to be crying. He asked them the reason of their trouble, and they told him that his own wife had that day killed their chief, the Yellow Rattlesnake, and they were just now about to send the Black Rattlesnake to take revenge.

The hunter said he was very sorry, but they told him that if he spoke the truth he must be ready to make satisfaction and give his wife as a sacrifice for the life of their chief. Not knowing what might happen otherwise, he consented. They then told him that the Black Rattlesnake would go home with him and coil up just outside the door in the dark. He must go inside, where he would find his wife awaiting him, and ask her to get him a drink of fresh water from the spring. That was all.

He went home and knew that the Black Rattlesnake was following. It was night when he arrived and very dark, but he found his wife waiting with his supper ready. He sat down and asked for a drink of water. She handed him a gourd full from the jar, but he said he wanted it fresh from the spring, so she took a bowl and went out of the door. The next moment he heard a cry, and going out he found that the Black Rattlesnake had bitten her and that she was already dying. He stayed with her until she was dead, when the Black Rattlesnake came out from the grass again and said his tribe was now satisfied.

He then taught the hunter a prayer song, and said, "When you meet any of us hereafter sing this song and we will not hurt you; but if by accident one of us should bite one of your people then sing this song over him and he will recover." And the Cherokee have kept the song to this day.

Hungry Mother

Deep in the Blue Ridge Highlands of Southwest Virginia is a state park that is over 5-square miles in size and features Appalachian woodland, a serene 108-acre lake, as well as mountain vistas that are second to none. This place is known as Hungry Mother Lake and for more than a quarter-century it has played host to a countless number of camping outings, family get-togethers, weddings, and happy memories too numerous to record.

Interestingly, the very name of this Virginia State Park speaks of grizzly tales in centuries past.

According to local legend, during the French and Indian War, unrest among the Native Americans and white settlers reached and all-time low and natives soon destroyed several settlements along the New River, south of the park in what is now Grayson County, Virginia.

Molly Marley and her small child were among the survivors taken to the raiders' base, which was located just north of the location of the park.

The pair eventually escaped, wandering through the wilderness eating berries and perhaps even tree-bark in order to sustain themselves.

Wearied from having been taken captive and attempting to walk back to safety while malnourished, Molly soon collapsed and died beside a small creek. The escaped duo were eventually found by an English search party and the only words the child would utter while lying next to his dead mother were, "Hungry Mother."

The creek was later named Hungry Mother Creek where, according to local legend, on full moon nights or at dusk on Halloween, you can still hear the child's cry coming from the woods near the creek, "hungry mother, hungry mother."

Ivanhoe: The Place Cursed by Robert Sheffey

In an age of fancy-pants televangelists, soft-spoken ministers and almost cartoonish local clergy, it might be difficult for the average American to understand that not too long ago, there was a sect of preachers who feared neither man nor beast, but were intimidating to even the most brazen of moonshiners.

Standing head and shoulders above most, these fearless men of God braved terrifying storms, endured hunger and battled deadly gangs at nearly every turn, simply in order to fulfill their calling to "faithfully execute the Scriptures."

These men were known as circuit riding preachers and the mark they have left upon the Appalachian mountains — and far beyond — will endure for an eternity.

Recalling his childhood memories of seeing these men firsthand, Edward Eggleston wrote, "More than anyone else, the early circuit preachers brought order out of this chaos. In no other class was the real heroic element so finely displayed. Oh how I remember the forms and weather-beaten visages of the old preachers, whose constitutions had conquered starvation and exposure — who had survived swamps, alligators, Indians, highway robbers and bilious fevers! How was my boyish soul tickled with their anecdotes of rude experience – how was my imagination wrought upon by the recital of their hair-breadth escapes! How was my heart set afire by their contagious religious enthusiasm…"

Back in an era when "The Wild West" was Tennessee, Kentucky and Ohio, frontier life was lonely. Cabins were often separated by miles and sparse population densities meant that churches, once a pillar of American society, were few and far between.

Seeking to meet the religious needs of the nation's frontier settlers, hundreds of brave preachers answered a call to roam from town to town throughout the "West" preaching the Gospel of a coming Christ.

Known as "saddlebag preachers" these frontier traveling clergymen set out on horseback, roaming through the wilderness, preaching each day in tiny villages, rural court houses, fields, meeting houses and even in the homes of settlers.

Many circuits were so large that it would take 5 to 6 weeks for the preacher to make a single lap, ministering to dozens of tiny congregations along the way.

The work of these traveling preachers is in part credited for the Bible Belt's very existence and as the country grew, so did the influence of these Daniel Boone-style preachers.

Seeking neither fame nor money, these zealous wilderness pastors soon grew into a mighty army for the Lord of heaven. In 1784, there were 83 traveling preachers. By 1839, their rank had swelled to 3,557.

In addition to being an immensely lonely profession, the work of an 18th century wilderness preacher was among the most perilous of professions a man could pursue.

Samuel Wakefield wrote a hymn about the perils circuit riders faced. It describes the circuit rider's family anxiously waiting for his return, only to learn that he had died in a far-away wilderness. The final stanza says:

Yet still they look with glistening eye,
Till lo! a herald hastens nigh;
He comes the tale of woe to tell,
How he, their prop and glory fell;
How died he in a stranger's room,
How strangers laid him in the tomb,
How spoke he with his latest breath,
And loved and blessed them all in death.

Fiercely independent, rugged and filled with conviction, circuit riding preachers of the 1800's attained a great reputation for being strong and unyielding men.

Staunchly opposed to liquor, stories abound of traveling ministers leading powerful prayers for the immediate destruction of whiskey stills and distilleries.

Some men involved in the whiskey distilling business are said to have gone so far as to flee an area rather than become the object of the prayers of circuit riding preachers.

Of the tens of thousands of circuit riders to traverse the wilderness countryside over the years, there is one name in Appalachia that is remembered above all the others: Robert Sheffey.

Born in the Ivanhoe community of Wythe County, Virginia, Robert Sheffey became orphaned at a very young age and was forced to move to nearby Abingdon, Virginia, to be raised by his aunt.

Sheffey would later say that he was "born of the flesh on July 4, 1820, in Ivanhoe, Wythe County, Virginia, and that he was born of the Spirit on January 9, 1839, over Greenway's store, at Abingdon, Virginia."

It was on this blustering January day that Sheffey heeded Jesus' call of "Ye must be born again…"

Asking Christ to be his personal Savior, Sheffey soon surrendered his life to full-time ministry and the same autumn, he enrolled into Emory & Henry College.

Unfortunately Sheffey's "early dislike for books and an aversion for profound study," made him a terrible student and the new believer soon dropped out of seminary altogether.

With no degree, but convinced of a heavenly calling on his life, Sheffey attempted to become ordained by the Methodist Church; however, his ordination was shot down due to his lack of education.

With no official ordination or formal degree, Sheffey set out into the hills and hollers of Appalachia as an itinerant preacher, circuit riding on horseback — roaming from town to town holding tent meetings and preaching a message of repentance.

His lack of education did in no wise affect his ability to faithfully minister and in fact one could conclude that it was this very trait that endeared him to the common man.

Many stories about Sheffey relating to his power in prayer abound. Some of his prayers concerned critical needs of agricultural communities, such as the need for rain in time of drought or the prevention of rain during harvest. Other of his prayers centered upon his disdain for alcohol.

According to an expert in the folklore of itinerant Methodist preachers, there are "at least twenty-five accounts of how Sheffey's prayers led to the immediate destruction of whiskey stills and distilleries."

According to one minister, Sheffey prayed for the destruction of three distilleries on a creek near where they had been preaching. The minister claimed the proprietor of one still, in robust health, died suddenly; at a second, Sheffey prayed that a tree would fall on the still house though there were no trees nearby, and a "great storm came and actually landed a tree on the still"; and a third still was destroyed by fire after Sheffey had spent a night in prayer against it.

Interestingly, there was one community that despite all of Sheffey's prayers and preaching would not repent and that was the very village in which he was born, Ivanhoe, Virginia.

But Jesus, said unto them, A prophet is not without honour, but in his own country, and among his own kin, and in his own house. – Mark 6.4

One local resident stated, "after weeks of unsuccessful preaching and

MOUNTAIN SUPERSTITIONS, GHOST STORIES & HAIN TALES

Photo: The Ivanhoe blast furnace. This blast furnace near the New River closed down in shortly after 1910.

praying, Sheffey concluded that the people of Ivanhoe did not have any desire to come to the Lord and that the town which was filled with whorehouses, drunkenness and fight'n had made its choice."

Fulfilling what was his interpretation of the Scriptures regarding a community that rejects the Gospel, Sheffey is said to have turned his back on the people on his ride out of town and dusted his shoes:

And whosoever shall not receive you, nor hear you, when ye depart thence, shake off the dust under your feet for a testimony against them. Verily I say unto you, It shall be more tolerable for Sodom and Gomorrha in the day of judgment, than for that city.
— Mark 6.11

A Wythe County historian writes, "Sheffey then cursed the community on his way out of town and said, 'Ivanhoe will never amount to a damn.' The preacher vowed to never step foot in Ivanhoe again and condemned the place to sink into the earth and be consumed by the pits of hell."

In the century that followed, Ivanhoe, Virginia's population would decline sharply and what was once a thriving community would experience heartache and pain on a tragic level as poverty would inflict the people as mines would close and an industrial park would never get off the ground.

Locals refer to the century of misfortune as Sheffey's curse – a belief that has gained traction in recent years as sinkholes have become a major problem in the area.

Despite blaming his curse for their problems, locals in Ivanhoe speak his name in a reverence that is reserved for none other. The local elementary school is named Sheffey Elementary School and his tombstone simply reads, "The poor were sorry when he died."

The Christmas Devil

Photo: A St. Nicholas procession with Krampus, and other characters, c. 1910

Christmas as we know it, with the giving of presents, mistletoe, and jolly o'le Saint Nic have been centuries in the making and have evolved with our ever changing culture.

Long before the birth of Rudolph the Red Nosed Reindeer in 1939, and even before December 25th became the internationally recognized day of Christmas, a cranky devilish creature known as Krampus was also making a list and checking it twice.

While the children of ancient days relished in the thought of Saint Nicholas passing by their way with a visit, bringing toys and candies for good little boys and girls, the dreams of many children from days past were also scarred with fears of a visit from this half-goat, half-demon monster who was believed to have accompanied Santa on his worldwide journey.

While Santa was busy giving good gifts to all the nice children, Krampus would be raining terror upon the children who had misbehaved that year — many legends say he carried a whip in his hands and a basket strapped to his back; this is to cart off evil children for drowning, eating, or transport to Hell.

Pretty hardcore eh?

The belief in Krampus actually predates Christianity and has its roots in early Germanic pagan religion; however, as Christmas and Santa rose in prominence throughout Europe, the people of these regions found a way to marry their ancient pre-Christian beliefs to that of Christmas.

Christmas was a holiday forbidden in many early-American colonies for its revelries, however, as the holiday found its way into American culture, early promoters of the holiday made great attempts to block Santa's sidekick, Krampus, entry into the nation.

However, the onset of the Industrial Revolution brought a tidal wave of new immigrants into America, including those who maintained belief in a goat-devil Christmas creature.

Many of these immigrants found work in the steel mills and coal mines and soon, interest in the Christmas Devil reached the point that newspapers in nation found themselves explaining the story of Krampus for those who found his entire myth fascinatingly frightening.

In 1907, the *Pittsburgh Post-Gazette* published an extensive article on Krampus, stating, "It is an old legend in Austria that St. Nicholas comes on December 6, accompanied by a devil on one side and an angel on the other, and visits all the children. The angel picks out the good children, and St. Nicholas leaves toys for them, and the devil, Krampus, as he is called, whips the naughty one with his willow switch and binds them with a chain. You would think that, being a devil, he would like the bad children best and punish only the good ones, but he must be a sort of reformed devil, or he wouldn't be going about with good St. Nicholas."

In the years ahead, the Krampus tradition would become prohibited throughout much of Europe, with governments distributing pamphlets arguing, "Krampus is an Evil Man".

Photo: A 1900s greeting card reading 'Greetings from Krampus!'

Apparently, Krampus was even considered too evil by Adolph Hitler and the Nazis, as the Nazis banned his celebration in Germany; however, as one writer stated, "Krampus never completely disappeared! He lurked in the shadows and always seemed to bounce back at different times in history!"

Today, there is a resurgence of Krampus tradition and interest... I'm sure a psychologist could have a field day explaining why this is the case!

—*Part Three*—
All Hallow's Eve In The Mountains

W. Va. Newspaper Account of Halloween 1898

West Virginia's The Wheeling Intelligencer, November 1, 1898, made the following report the morning after Halloween. The report provides an interesting glimpse into the typical mischief a mountain community experienced Halloween night in the late 1800s.

HEADLINE:
Halloween Kept `the Police Force Very Busy Last Evening

The observance of Halloween last night was general, to say the least, and prosperity was evident judging by the kids, who played late and loose with rice.

No wedding couple ever was showered with more rice as some law-abiding citizen's doorsteps. "There was abundance of corn in Egypt," if the amount spread on the pavements was any indication.

The small boy is a come-to-the-front individual at all times, except it be when school bells ring, but he was on land, in all his glory last night.

The ubiquitous kid was here, there, and everywhere, and the police were kept busy. Door bells rung, doors were hammered at, rates were lifted from their hinges and the old-time Halloween pranks were carried on, just the same as they were years ago.

Viewed from social X-rays the occasion was more than of ordinary note. The taffy-pullin's were especially conspicuous, in all the wards the odor of the succulent concoction was borne of the dying October night breezes. It was social festivity.

Inside the house, and small boy activity outside, that deadly weapon, the bean-shooter, rent havoc. And then came the ticktack and others.

Halloween of 1898 received all the honors due the occasion, and if nothing else it will go on record is a howling success.

The Night Charleston Panicked

On the evening of Sunday, October 30, 1938, dozens of emergency management agencies across the nation found themselves working overtime as many Americans were set into a panic following the radio broadcast of H.G. Wells' "War of the Worlds."

Aired as a Halloween special, the radio broadcast caught many unsuspecting American families off guard, as outlandish claims of an alien attack upon the federal government were aired in a seemingly real manner.

The program began with an uneventful and ordinary orchestra rendition; however, in the opening minutes of the evening broadcast there was a short interruption for a special "news bulletin," which stated that a cylindrical meteorite had landed in a farm field in New Jersey.

As the evening progressed, however, the news bulletins became more detailed. Soon, radio reporter Carl Philips was describing a crowd that had gathered around the crash site.

First he announced that the cylinder had unscrewed.

Next, onlookers were heard "catching a glimpse of a tentacled, pulsating, barely mobile Martian inside."

Moments later, Phillips and the entire crowd were incinerated by alien heat-rays. Phillips' shouts about incoming flames were cut off in mid-sentence.

To the listener, it seemed that regular programming broke down as the network struggled with casualty updates and firefighting developments.

The broadcast featured a shaken newsman speculating about Martian technology, as well as an update pertaining to the New Jersey state militia's implementation of martial law. A message from the militia's "field headquarters" begged listeners to remain calm and assured them that the American military was properly equipped to handle an alien invasion; moments later, the Martians were reported to have obliterated the militia.

As the night progressed, the network ran numerous news bulletins giving damage reports and evacuation instructions to what it claimed were millions of refugees attempting to leave the state of New Jersey. An unnamed "Secretary of the Interior" addressed the nation and actor Kenny Delmar's voice, which was closely similar to President Franklin D. Roosevelt's, also advised the nation to maintain order.

With each passing minute, the program grew more and more bizarre.

Hundreds of miles to the southwest, West Virginia's capital city of Charleston was sent into an uproar, as terrified residents mistook the nationally syndicated broadcast to be the real deal!

One local newspaper reported, "The broadcast play led hundreds of Charleston residents to think [that it was a real alien attack], and they anxiously inquired for news dispatches and hastily prepared to flee to the hills."

Charlestonians were not alone in their misguided fears. The broadcast's producer, John Houseman, noticed that at about 8:32 pm. ET, CBS supervisor Davidson Taylor received a telephone call in the control room. Creasing his lips, Taylor left the studio and returned four minutes later, "pale as death", as he had been ordered to interrupt "The War of the Worlds" broadcast immediately with an announcement of the program's fictional content. But by the time the order was given, the program was already less than a minute away from its first scheduled break, and the fictional news reporter played by actor Ray Collins was choking on poison gas as the Martians overwhelmed New York.

Actor Stefan Schnabel recalled sitting in the anteroom after finishing his on-air performance. "A few policemen trickled in, then a few more. Soon, the room was full of policemen and a massive struggle was going on between the police, page boys, and CBS executives, who were trying to prevent the cops from busting in and stopping the show. It was a show to witness."

During the sign-off theme, the phone began ringing. Houseman picked it up and the furious caller announced he was mayor of a Midwestern town where mobs were in the streets. Houseman hung up quickly: "We were off the air now and the studio door had burst open."

"The following hours were a nightmare. The building was suddenly full of people and dark-blue uniforms. Hustled out of the studio, we were locked into a small back office on another floor. Here we sat incommunicado while network employees were busily collecting, destroying, or locking up all scripts and records of the broadcast. Finally, the Press was let loose upon us, ravening for horror. How many deaths had we heard of? (Implying they knew of thousands.) What did we know of the fatal stampede in a Jersey hall? (Implying it was one of many.) What traffic deaths? (The ditches must be choked with corpses.) The suicides? (Haven't you heard about the one on Riverside Drive?) It is all quite vague in my memory and quite terrible." wrote John Houseman in his memoir in 1972.

Paul White, head of CBS News, was quickly summoned to the office – "and there bedlam reigned", he wrote:

"The telephone switchboard, a vast sea of light, could handle only a fraction of incoming calls. The haggard Welles sat alone and despondent. 'I'm through,' he lamented, 'washed up.' I didn't bother to reply to this highly inaccurate self-appraisal. I was too busy writing explanations to put on the air, reassuring the audience that it was safe. I also answered my share of incessant telephone calls, many of them from as far away as the Pacific Coast."

Back in Charleston, West Virginia, panic reigned at "city and state police headquarters, at newspapers and at radio station WCHS [which] groaned under the inquiries... State troopers took time off to reassure a weeping mother that she and her children were safe."

One man was rushed to a downtown hospital in Charleston, after fainting while listening to the broadcast.

Another incident alleges that a police officer was summoned to his home by short wave radio.

When the officer arrived home, "He found his uncle, greatly alarmed, headed for the drug store, where he was going to stock up on an antidote for mustard gas. It took several minutes to dissuade him and convince him that there was no immediate danger of gas attack."

According to Jefferson Pooley, a few suicide attempts were made that evening. The Washington Post claimed that a man died of a heart attack brought on by listening to the program and one woman filed a lawsuit against CBS, but it was soon dismissed.

On November 2, 1938, the Australian Age characterized the incident as "mass hysteria" and stated that "never in the history of the United States had such a wave of terror and panic swept the continent."

Dingess Tunnel

The History of the Dingess Tunnel

Hidden deep within the coal filled Appalachian Mountains of Southern West Virginia rests a forgotten land that is older than time itself. Its valleys are deep, its waters polluted and its terrain is as rough as the rugged men and women who have occupied these centuries old plats for thousands of years.

The region is known as "Bloody Mingo" and for decades the area has been regarded as one of the most murderous areas in all of American history.

The haunted mountains of this region have been the stage of blood baths too numerous to number, including those of the famed Hatfield's and McCoy's, Matewan Massacre and the Battle of Blair Mountain.

Tucked away in a dark corner of this remote area is an even greater anomaly – a town, whose primary entrance is a deserted one lane train tunnel nearly 4/5 of a mile long.

The story of this town's unique entrance dates back nearly a century and a half ago, back to an era when coal mining in West Virginia was first becoming profitable.

For generations, the people of what is now Mingo County, West Virginia, had lived quiet and peaceable lives, enjoying the fruits of the land, living secluded within the tall and unforgiving mountains surrounding them.

All of this changed, however, with the industrial revolution, as the demand for coal and timber soared to record highs.

Soon outside capital began flowing into "Bloody Mingo" and within a decade railroads had linked the previously isolated communities of southern West Virginia to the outside world.

The most notorious of these new railways was Norfolk & Western's line between Lenore and Wayne County – a railroad that split through the hazardous and lawless region known as "Twelve Pole Creek."

At the heart of Twelve Pole Creek, railroad workers forged a 3,300 foot long railroad tunnel just south of the community of Dingess.

As new mines began to open, destitute families poured into Mingo County in search of labor in the coal mines. Among the population of workers were large numbers of African-Americans.

Despising outsiders, and particularly the thought of dark skinned people moving into what had long been viewed as a region exclusively all their own, residents of Dingess, West Virginia, are said to have hid along the hillsides just outside of the tunnel's entrance, shooting any dark skinned travelers riding aboard the train.

Though no official numbers were ever kept, a countless number of black workers are said to have been killed at the entrance and exits of this tunnel.

As a little boy, I remember sitting at my late-grandmother's feet, just a few miles north of the infamous Dingess Tunnel in Mingo County, West Virginia, listening to her tell tales of the area's murderous and lawless history.

She once told me that when she was not very many more years older than I was — I was probably ten at the time — that she witnessed a murder while in the mountains taking a walk. Her court testimony ended up being enough to find the individual guilty and she spent many years worrying of retribution.

As I grew older, I realized that tales abounded of the county's infamy, so much so that it was known throughout the state as "Bloody Mingo." The stories ranged from late-night lynchings, to dead bodies being hanged from the tunnel's ceiling.

I'm reluctant to believe every story I hear about this tunnel, simply because it's in human nature to sometimes exaggerate a good story and this area begs for a great stories to be told; however, at the same time, I've spent a lot of time "on" Dingess (not "in") and I can say for a fact that many of these stories are true.

Huey Perry, author of *They'll Cut Off Your Project*, wrote, "Old-timers there said it was common practice to have a killing once a month. As 'Uncle' Jim Marcum described it, 'Why, a colored person couldn't think about riding through Dingess. They would stop the train, take him off and shoot him, and nobody would say a word. Why, they would even stop the train and take all its cargo. It was a wild country then, and it ain't much better now.'"

According to Perry, from 1900 to 1972, approximately seventeen lawmen were shot to death in the area which stretches fifteen miles along Twelve Pole Creek.

Not very many years after digging the tunnel and establishing the Twelve Pole line, Norfolk & Western abandoned the tracks – soon silence reigned in the rugged mountains overlooking the area. Gone were the whistles of locomotives and the rumble of cars. Nothing but long, winding bed of cinders, a few decayed ties, and several steel bridges remained.

For decades the skeletal remains of Norfolk & Western's failed railway line stood as a silent testimony to the region's ghostly ways.

In the early 1960's, however, the resourceful men of the mountains commandeered the former railroad line and built upon its beds a road for motorists to travel upon.

Unfortunately, residents of this impoverished region failed to secure funding from the state's legislature to improve the tunnel and bridges, thus today – over half a century later – residents of this community are forced to drive atop countless one lane train bridges and a nearly mile long one lane tunnel.

For residents of this community, such a drive is just another part of their daily routine, however, for visitors unfamiliar with the thought of driving through a one lane tunnel with a fifty ton coal truck at the other end, such an experience can be heart pounding to say the least.

One writer said the following of his experience driving through the

Dingess Tunnel:

"Locals state that proper usage is to turn lights on, indicating that you are entering the tunnel. Drivers from the other end know not to enter if lights are on. We saw an 18 wheeler tanker go through while there, but it is a tight fit. Water drips from the top and one can barely see as it takes a while for eyes to adjust. Locals state that the roadway was dirt up until a couple of years ago and had deep holes in it. Now it is paved, but no lighting."

A Series of Tragedies

In addition to being scene of snipers killing train passengers, the tunnel also experienced its share of tragedies in the form of workplace accidents and train crashes over the short time it was used for train traffic.

In 1898 a fatal train wreck in the tunnel killed seven people.

Seven years later in 1905, tragedy struck again when a fully loaded freight train collided head on with a work train. This accident left another three people dead.

In addition to being the site of numerous murders and railway deaths, the area's isolation created a standing invitation for thieves and train hijackers.

The following news article appeared in the November 23, 1901, edition of the *Bluefield Daily Telegraph*:

"A report has just reached here to the effect that burglars made a raid on the town of Dingess, on the Kenova division early Thursday morning, and visited various business houses and residences.

"It was not until they had dynamited a large safe that their presence became known. Citizens were on the scene almost immediately after the heavy report, and the burglars hadn't time to gather up their booty as a number of citizens opened fire and probably forty shots were exchanged. The burglars, who secured a lot of valuable jewelry, escaped on a hand car which was recovered later four miles from Dingess, and on which blood spots were plainly visible.

"A clerk in the Greer store was shot in the arm, but not seriously injured.

"It is believed that the robbers are headed for Huntington, and the police of that city have been notified to keep on the lookout for them."

Dingess on Halloween Night

My father, his mother, and his grandparents all grew up in this storied community and as memory recalls, on Halloween night, Dingess was the very last place in West Virginia any outsider desired to be.

I remember my mother actually going so far as to reschedule a planned visit "back home", when I was a kid, once she realized that she'd be in

"Bloody Mingo" during the week of Halloween.

Though the world has done its best to tame this free spirited community, only a handful of years ago, Halloween night brought with it untamed and unrivaled mischief.

For no other reason than the excitement of wrongdoing, many of the young men of the community would set fire to tires inside the tunnel every Halloween night — an action that would greatly complicate travel into and out of this West Virginia community.

After the main entrance to the tiny hamlet had been successfully blocked off by the deadly cocktail of melted rubber and blazing tires, a combination which emitted smoke so poisonous and black the tunnel would be closed for the remainder of the night and well into the week, the partiers would then move to the side roads, where only the largest of trees would be sawed down and made to fall onto the roadways beneath in an effort to bring additional lawlessness to an area already prone to mischief.

Further tomfoolery would be brought to the community as teenagers would then engage in uninhabited devilry — ranging from throwing rocks through windows to setting fire to vehicles and structures.

When asked about her memories of Halloween, Ruth Sturgill Preece of Mingo County offered this statement to *Appalachian Magazine*, "We dressed up in homemade costumes and played pranks on each other... We all enjoyed walking together in a group... There was just happiness, plus candy! And back then, there was no cutting trees across the road to block traffic... later on in years they started cutting trees and set fires in the tunnel and destruction of property. If we had done that we would have gotten a switch and no more trick or treat. Back then the churches still frowned on Halloween anyway..."

Today, things in this area have calmed down considerably, but folks still remember the days when October 31 more closely resembled the night of a real life "Purge" movie than an innocent evening of trick or treating!

Thanks for Reading!
Check out another Appalachian Magazine publication

Appalachian Magazine's Mountain Voice 2017 serves as an exhaustive collection of published online articles showcasing the Memories, Histories, and Tall Tales of life in Appalachia. Containing over eighty heart-warming and thought provoking stories of "down home", the publication takes readers on a timeless journey through the Central Appalachian Mountains. Readers will explore the rich traditions of mountain religion, visit forgotten landmarks, be reminded of ancient mountain superstitions, debate the validity of tall tales and mountain legends, as well as explore new ideas and concepts for an ever changing Appalachian region. Launched by Appalachian natives Jeremy and Allison Farley, the magazine has been a labor of love for the couple and readers can expect for Appalachian Magazine's Mountain Voice 2017 to be merely the first of several dozens of years' worth of printed annual publications aimed at highlighting the history and life of the mountains of home... That is, Lord willing... and the creeks don't rise!

Amazon Review – 4.5 / 5 Starts

Available for purchase on Amazon.com

Made in the USA
Middletown, DE
07 August 2024